Stepping Out on Faith

How to Open a Quality Childcare Center

By

Deborah L. Tillman, M.S. Ed

authorHOUSE™

1663 LIBERTY DRIVE, SUITE 200
BLOOMINGTON, INDIANA 47403
(800) 839-8640
WWW.AUTHORHOUSE.COM

First published by AuthorHouse 03/01/05

ISBN: 1-4208-0141-4 (e)
ISBN: 1-4208-1004-9 (sc)

Printed in the United States of America
Bloomington, Indiana

This book is printed on acid-free paper.

This book is dedicated to my son ZEPLYN,

the one who started the train.

And to all the mothers who believe that they **can** *do it better.*

You may not think you can reach it…

Climb anyway

You may not think you'll be heard…

Speak anyway

You may not think you can change things…

Try anyway

~ Maya Angelou

TABLE OF CONTENTS

INTRODUCTION ix

LABOR AND DELIVERY 1

PROVIDER #1 4

PROVIDER #2 6

PROVIDER #3 10

PROVIDER #4 13

PROVIDER #5 15

PROVIDER #6 17

PROVIDER #7 19

CHOICES 21

ARE YOU READY? 24

PLANNING 26

LICENSING REQUIREMENTS 28

DEVELOPING POLICIES BASED ON REQUIREMENTS 30

STAFFING 31

CURRICULUM DEVELOPMENT 33

ROOM ARRANGEMENT AND DESIGN 41

FOOD AND NUTRITION 46

DEVELOPING A FINANCIAL PLAN 48

DEVELOPING A MARKETING PLAN 50

CONCLUSION 55

Appendix A Sample Parent Handbook 57

Appendix B Sample Employee Handbook 83

Appendix C List of Resources 105

INTRODUCTION

Writing this book has not only been an arduous process and an enlightening experience, but also therapeutic. As I reviewed the scribbled pages of my diary and deciphered the thoughts that went through my mind with each childcare provider, I wondered why I didn't see that God was working His wondrous plan for me from the very beginning. Why did it take me seven horrifying experiences to realize that? I wouldn't wish what happened to me and my young son on anyone.

My situation happened and most likely needed to happen in order for me to find my true purpose in life. Was it a challenge? Yes. Was it often frustrating? Yes. Was I fearful? NO, because God does not give us the spirit of fear when He shows us our purpose. We instantly know and realize that all things work together for good to them who love God and to them who are called according to His purpose (**Romans 8:28**).

After I was featured in the October 2002 issue of ***Essence* magazine**, I was inundated with thousands of telephone calls, e-mails, and letters from teachers, providers, business owners, stay-at-home moms, and yes, dads, all wanting to know how to start, where to go first, and what to do.

I was already in the process of writing a book, but I had been procrastinating. The national exposure forced me to open up the file cabinets and dust off some of my notes and other materials in order to complete this book.

So, to the thousands of people who always wanted to open a childcare center, but were told that they couldn't do it, this one's for you. My only hope is that after you read this book, you will be inspired to stop talking, stop procrastinating, and stop living in fear. Stop and take the *t* out of CAN'T and replace it with CAN. Begin to think, eat, love, do, be, and **LIVE YOUR PURPOSE**. You will be happy that you did.

I must give thanks and praise to God. Without HIM, none of this would have been possible. My deepest gratitude to my spiritual parents Pastor Lyle Dukes and Co-Pastor Deborah Dukes of the Harvest Life Changers Church, International for teaching and preaching the unadulterated Word of God. Thanks to my mother, the teacher, whom I have watched give her three daughters the strength, love, guidance, and determination to get through anything. Thanks to my father, who gave me so much self-confidence that I had to learn how to channel it. Thanks to my grandparents, who made me more humble. Thanks to my godfather, who showed me what working hard could really bring you. Thanks to my sisters for being my best friends. Finally, thanks to my husband, who allowed me to cry, and to our son, Zeplyn, who was the train, the inspiration, and the beginning to a wonderful life of working with our nation's most precious "little ones" … our children.

LABOR AND DELIVERY

As I lay awake in the bed, I remembered hearing the doctor say to me that I would know when it was time, that I would feel a sensation unlike any other. The television in the living room was loud enough to make my mind jump like a leaping frog. As the surging pressure in my abdomen became more frequent, I called out. Well, it was more like a SHOUT OUT to my husband. "Come quickly," I said. He didn't respond. I repeated myself, "James, come quickly." Why wasn't he responding? I made a third feeble attempt to get his attention, but to no avail. I took a deep breath and began to roll over onto my side.

The feeling had subsided for a brief moment, and as it did, I slowly got up and walked into the living room, where my dear husband was sleeping. How could he be sleeping with all of the ruckus from the television? I reached deep down and screamed his name. I was not angry with him, but a sensation took over my body again in a way unlike anything I had ever experienced. He jumped up and said, "Is it time?" Somehow, I must have missed the session of Lamaze that taught one not to be angry, but to be kind. "What do you mean is it time? I have been calling you for the past ten minutes," I screamed.

He seemed totally unaffected by my sudden outburst. Perhaps he was used to the mood swings that made me look like, seem like, and transform into a person I didn't even like. Thank God for all of the "good" husbands who have the patience to withstand and endure. Know that you are a blessing. Unfortunately, we can only realize that in hindsight.

James walked over to the table to call my physician. Once he pushed the speakerphone button, my physician began asking a series of questions. How far apart are the pains? How many? He instructed my husband to time the contractions. He indicated that when they got to be less than five minutes apart, we should go to the hospital. He also contended that I should remember my breathing techniques. *Survival technique* is more appropriate to use. After approximately fifty minutes, we anxiously headed to the hospital. The bags had been packed since early spring.

It was now the evening of June 3rd. What had proven to be one of my most painful life experiences had turned out to be one of the best things that ever happened to me. My whole perspective on life changed during those seven hours of labor. At 3:05 AM, on June 4th, God blessed us with a healthy, nine-pound, eight-ounce baby boy named Zeplyn Xavier Tillman.

A baby, how lovely he can be. However, motherhood can be quite lonely and depressing. In retrospect, I believe that I was going through a stage of depression. During the first month after the baby arrived, I was overwhelmed with the huge responsibility of caring for this little life. I stayed up late nursing. I was extremely exhausted due to the extra sixty pounds of weight I gained over the last four months.

The state of not being "in control" was alarming to me. I didn't tell anyone about my feelings, except God. He is the only one I can turn to in my times of worry and despair. He can lead, guide, and direct my path in ways that are unimaginable. I noticed that the more I prayed, stayed in the word, and trusted in God, the more the feelings subsided. Over the next few weeks, I grew closer to Zeplyn, and we began to bond. At times, I felt I could burst with so many feelings of love, joy, and happiness. The love that one feels for a child is different from any other love. This was for the first time in my life that I would sacrifice my own life for his. I wondered if this was how I was supposed to feel.

I was on my sixth week of maternity leave with only six weeks left before having to return to work. I was a staff accountant at an engineering company where I had worked for almost two years. I was twenty-nine years old, made over $33,000, and received a significant amount in bonuses each year that was enough money to feed a family of three for at least a few months. What was I to do? I loved being with my son, but I felt I needed to work outside of the home because I enjoyed a challenge. Despite popular belief, being a good homemaker or stay-at-home mom is very taxing. It takes determination, perseverance, and a significant amount of versatility on the part of the parent. You also have to be prepared for it. Everything is done at a faster pace. It was much easier for me to continue working the field of Corporate America.

My husband and I began the grueling task of finding reliable, quality childcare for our son. We discussed what we wanted and who a prime candidate would be. First, we considered childcare centers. However, in the city of Alexandria, there were not many to choose from. And, centers we did visit had no immediate space available. I began asking why I waited so long to begin my search. I should have started looking when I was expecting. However, in my divine wisdom, I have learned not to question too much. If it is in God's plan for your life, then it is uniquely scripted from the beginning to end and will work out just the way it should.

Next, we looked at in-home childcare providers. We obtained a long list from the Department of Social Services and went through the providers who were licensed by the city and the state. Then we lined up interviews in the evening. We didn't want the providers to be taken away from their busy daily schedules with the children to visit with us. We respected the positions of providers who affected the lives of children each day. The process was slow and sometimes painful. We visited the homes and apartments of some who sounded promising on the phone, only to find that their places of residence were filthy. I wondered how and why anyone could leave his or her child there. Time has always been a valuable commodity to me, so I didn't waste it. We never stayed to interview those providers. I felt that if their homes looked despicable, how could the children be cared for?

Finally, after our nineteenth interview, we received a reference from a woman who worked in the office of my son's pediatrician. She said her son went to this woman, and she described her as "an older grandma type" who treated the children in her care with much love and respect. After our initial meeting with her, we asked to come by to see how she worked with the children. Since she did not object, we showed up at the front door on Monday morning at 10:00. She was the only woman in the room. There were four children and one assistant; her second assistant had not arrived yet.

Mrs. Mitchell had been married for forty-eight years. She was older, but moved swiftly and seemed to be very kind to the children. While in the living room, we heard a baby crying. She immediately excused herself to see what the problem was—a good sign. She was attentive, kind, and very loving to the children. She answered another series of questions very well. We stayed until breakfast was over then left. We decided to wait twenty-four hours before making a decision. We thought about our two visits with her. It was the "little" things that helped us to decide to pick her. However, my best impression was the feeling I got when in her presence. After all, she didn't seem like a person who would hurt or abuse a child.

PROVIDER #1

It was September 4, 1992, and Zeplyn was about to embark upon his three-month-old birthday. He was a very quiet child who only cried when he needed something or wanted to be held. He wore an outfit that had been given to him by his godmother. It was a brisk morning, so we wrapped up tightly. I decided not to return to work until the following week. This gave me an opportunity to be available if he was having a difficult time. As we drove up to Mrs. Mitchell's house, I reminisced about the night before: packing diapers and wipes, and preparing bottles and clothes for his first big day. I remembered feelings of guilt and wondered if we were making the right choice or whether we had rushed the process.

Whatever I may have been feeling was nothing compared to the feeling that took over my body when I dropped him off. I turned off the car and sat quietly thinking about how I was going to be strong enough to leave my baby with a stranger. I began to pray and ask God for the strength I needed. Ask and it shall be given; seek and you shall find. Did I know what I was asking for? Just then, I heard a knock on the window. It was Mrs. Mitchell, who had come outside to greet us. She smiled and said, "The first few weeks are always hard, my dear. However, Zeplyn will be just fine." Somehow, deep down I did know that he would be fine and that God would be there for him always. I kissed Zeplyn goodbye and gave Mrs. Mitchell a long list of emergency numbers and instructions on feeding times, mood swings, and changing times. Then tears started to stream down my face. I immediately drove to a nearby park and meditated. When I looked at the clock, it was three hours later.

I couldn't imagine leaving Zeplyn at Mrs. Mitchell's all day, so I picked him up at 12:35 PM. I didn't call before I came. An assistant opened the door and called for Mrs. Mitchell. Mrs. Mitchell came out of the bedroom with my three-month-old son in her arms. He had recently awakened from a nap. She said, "Oh, Zeplyn. Here is Mommy. Let's go over and see Mommy." She walked close to me, and I saw the sparkle in his eyes. I knew that he had a good first day.

The next couple of days went smoothly until I began to notice that Zeplyn's diapers were soaked when I got home. When I spoke to Mrs. Mitchell about the diapers, she became very defensive. She said that his diapers were wet because I lived twenty-five minutes from her house, and he must have been wetting his diaper on the way home. I didn't argue with her, but I did insist that she keep a chart of the times when he was changed. She said that's fine. For the next week, I received a chart, but he was still coming home wet. I noticed that the same times were marked the same each day (8:00 AM, 9:00, 10:30, 11:30, 12:15 PM, 3:30, 4:45, 5:15, and 5:45). I decided on Friday to take him at 8:30 AM and pick him up at 4:00 PM. Here was the problem. The times were still the same, showing that he was wet at 8:00 AM and 9:00 AM. When I questioned Mrs. Mitchell about the discrepancy, she became very defensive and agitated with me. I decided to disenroll Zeplyn.

Looking back, I know that I didn't disenroll him because of the wet diapers, but because her attitude frightened me. She was very defensive whenever asked a question. I thought to myself, how could someone not expect a mother to ask questions? Secondly, why would anyone get upset unless he or she had something to hide? Thank God my mother-in-law was visiting at the time. That gave me at least two weeks to find another childcare provider. We began interviewing more childcare providers. The search for the second provider seemed to come with much less pain. I think the search was less painful because I already knew what *not* to look for.

 PROVIDER #2

Mrs. Johnson was her name. She was referred to me by an acquaintance who had heard through the grapevine that I was looking for quality childcare. Mrs. Johnson was in her mid-forties. She had twelve years' experience and received excellent references. She cared for approximately three preschool children, and she didn't want any more than four children because she needed to be able to provide individual attention to each of them. Zeplyn would be her only four-month-old.

He started on a Monday and seemed very comfortable going to Mrs. Johnson. She smiled a lot and seemed very pleasant when I called during the day. I often wondered how Mrs. Johnson perceived me. I wondered if she saw me as a frantic first-time mother, who took twenty visits until I found a provider. Then once found, I would only stay for one month. I thought that if I continued to call throughout the day, she might think that I didn't trust her. She was taking time away from the children to speak to me. My phone calls were less than two minutes. Mrs. Johnson seemed nice and, for the first two weeks, catered to my son, especially when I arrived. She showed genuine concern for Zeplyn until the third week.

My place of employment had an electrical problem, and the supervisor let me go home early. I looked forward to the extra mommy/son time that I would be able to spend with him. It was approximately 11:30 AM. I was headed to pick up my son, whom I had dropped off at 7:00 AM. I thought about how we would spend time together. When I arrived at Mrs. Johnson's house, I rang the doorbell. I stood outside for about thirty seconds and rang again. I waited another minute and began to feel stomach knots. After two minutes, I started ringing and banging, thinking she was in the bathroom and didn't hear me. That thought was not consoling because if that were true, who would be watching the children?

After what seemed like ten minutes, but was closer to five, I called her home phone. At first, the answering machine came on and told me to leave a message. I just kept calling her name and asking her to open the door. I called her phone again. On the third ring, I heard her say, "I'm here; I'm coming." When she opened the door, I knew. Her hair and makeup were in disarray, and the first of her shirt buttons was fastened in the second buttonhole. It would have been noticeable to someone who had looked in the mirror prior to answering the door. However, from the looks of Mrs. Johnson, she had not seen a mirror. Many thoughts raced through my mind. Where was my son? I thought she told me Mr. Johnson was in California until the end of the week. I couldn't waste much time on that thought. I was actually speechless; anyone who knows me would think that is unimaginable. I stared at her for a brief moment, and then I pushed my way into her house.

I finally mustered up enough of my senses to ask what took her so long. She didn't answer. I asked, "Where is Zeplyn?" She pointed to the second room on the left. I ran into the room, and he was fortunately lying on the bed asleep. I was happy that he was not awake and unattended. Unfortunately, there were two three-year-old children sitting at a table with white paper and some broken crayons. Their noses were dirty, and one of the girls was crying. She kept saying, "I want my mommy." I looked at her and said to myself, "I want my mommy, too."

I don't think that I ever really appreciated the love and sacrifice that my mother gave to my two sisters and me until I became a mother. Our relationship always seemed strained while growing up. I viewed my older sister as the crème de la crème. Other family members nicknamed her "Little Lila," my mother's first name. My younger sister always got a lot of attention because she was the youngest and, I think, the most fragile. She was only months old when my mother and father separated. The strain in my relationship with my mother became more visible when my father left. I was a daddy's girl and, in some small way, blamed my mother for not making it work. It wasn't until I was much older that I realized my mother did the very best she could with the circumstances at hand. Her strength is remarkable. To be able to raise three beautiful daughters on very little money while working two, sometimes three, jobs is unimaginable. We didn't need for anything. God always provided. I learned about my mother's hard work and persistence at a young age. I realized that I couldn't blame my mother for the separation any more than I could blame my father. You get to a point in life when you have to take responsibility for yourself. So the little girl crying at the table reminded me of how much I wanted and needed my own mother to be here at this time. I wept with and for her.

A very tall, dark-skinned man appeared from the bedroom to ask the little girl what was wrong. Had he been in the bedroom the whole time? He didn't look like the man in the wedding picture with Mrs. Johnson on the mantle. Mrs. Johnson seemed to be very nervous. I couldn't understand why she wasn't speaking to the little girl. I grabbed my child's coat. I woke Zeplyn up and left. I was disheartened because she disappointed me. What was it with people leaving children unsupervised? Although those children at the table were not mine, they were someone else's children, and they needed to be cared for. People do not take their jobs seriously. Would it have mattered if the man who came out of the bedroom had been Mr. Johnson? Would that have made me less furious? I don't think so. I wasn't there to judge her morals, but I did wonder what she was teaching these young children who learn by example.

Regardless, I was at square one with no time to find another provider. I begged my mother-in-law to stay longer so that we could interview. Again, I was beginning to wonder if I was doing something wrong. Was I asking the proper questions? Why weren't these people who seemed to be quite nice not working out? My prayers were for God to show me the way and to let me know what I was supposed to do and to show me the person who was supposed to watch over my child. I couldn't understand at the time why my prayers were not being answered … or were they?

We began looking through the endless list sent from the Department of Social Services again, hoping that we may have overlooked a name before. At least Zeplyn would be with his grandmother, whom I trusted impeccably. I lined up interviews each day after work for a week.

We finally decided upon a woman who had been licensed recently by the city and the state. She said that she had three children and wanted to keep that number in order to give individual attention to each of them. She had wonderful references, and people spoke about her as if they really liked the way she cared for children. I observed her for two days from 9:00 AM to 12:30 PM with two other children. She appeared kind, patient, considerate, and loving. But then again, how else could she be with me watching her? I dropped by during the next few days unannounced, and she genuinely did not seem to mind. She said she didn't have anything to hide and that she just wanted me to be relaxed. She said she had experience with first-time mothers and that we were known to be overly cautious. She was right. I was overly everything. When I worried, I worried a lot about him.

I spent most of his waking moments when he was not in childcare with him. I fed him, bathed him, read to him, played with him, and put him to sleep. I truly loved it. I also know that I felt guilty for not being a stay-at-home mom. I often spent the early mornings with Zeplyn. After I picked him up from the sitter, I spent from 6:00 PM to around 8:00 PM with him. Thank God, my husband never complained about the amount of time I spent with my son until years later when things became difficult. I am glad that he didn't express his feelings at that time because of my state of mind. I wouldn't have been able to understand his point of view or have even wanted to.

PROVIDER #3

Mrs. Coleman was her name. She was the mother of a coworker. Her daughter talked about her as if she was the best thing since Mother Theresa. She was fifty-six years old and was watching two other children. She cared for one child in the morning and the other in the afternoon. If I used her as a childcare provider, my son would be the only full-time child. Perhaps I had found the one who would devote individual time to my child. Anyway, after the interview and observations, we chose Mrs. Coleman. She would start before my mother-in-law had to return to Florida.

The day was sunny, and I felt good. Zeplyn's bags were packed with diapers, bottles, and cereal. The first weeks went very well. Zeplyn seemed happy and content when I picked him up and dropped him off. When I picked him up early, not only was Zeplyn happy to see me, but Mrs. Coleman was as well. She was never defensive when I asked questions. She smiled a lot and seemed to love what she was doing. Could she finally be the one who would put my worries to ease? During the next few weeks, I was more productive at work. I didn't worry as much. She seemed like she didn't have anything to hide. During the third week, I fell behind on some work. I called to ask Mrs. Coleman if she could watch Zeplyn for an extra half-hour. When I arrived at Mrs. Coleman's house, the lights were out. When I rang the doorbell, Mrs. Coleman's daughter, Wilma, answered the door. She said that her mother had to go to the store and left Zeplyn with her. She said he finished his last bottle an hour before I arrived, so I put on his coat and carried him out to the car.

The next day at Mrs. Coleman's, she apologized for going to the store. She said that her daughter only watched Zeplyn for ten minutes before I arrived. She also stated that Zeplyn needed more bottles throughout the day. I had started with four bottles and cereal. Then two weeks later, we added two more bottles, and now she needed another two. I told her that he was only with her for ten hours a day maximum. I knew that he slept from 10:00 to 12:00 and then again from 3:30 to 5:00 PM. Why would he need so many bottles? She said that he was growing and it is always better to have more than less. She was older and, I thought, wiser. In addition, I didn't want to rock the boat, especially since she was taking care of my child. The thought of getting on the wrong side of a childcare provider was something that I didn't want to do for the fear of him being mistreated. So, I provided her with the extra bottles. Even though I included additional bottles, Zeplyn did not seem to be gaining any weight. In fact, he seemed to be losing weight.

After a couple more weeks and a doctor's appointment to validate my concerns, I asked Mrs. Coleman for a list of feeding times. Also, I asked whether the reports that indicated Zeplyn finished all ten bottles each day were actually correct or if he was only drinking half of the bottle. She said that he had been drinking his entire bottle, and she would provide me with a schedule of feeding times. Prior experience told me that the ramifications could be detrimental. Therefore, I had to prepare myself to start interviewing again, in case things didn't turn out as I had hoped.

During the next day at work, Mrs. Coleman's daughter, Wilma, did not speak, and she seemed agitated. After 12:30 PM, I couldn't take it anymore and asked her what the problem was. She responded, "You don't know?" I know that my face had a puzzled expression on it. She said, "Why would you tell my mother that she is not feeding your child? My mother has never had anyone question her. If she said that ten bottles was not enough, then you just need to bring more." She ended by saying that her mother did not need the extra aggravation, and she didn't have to provide me with feeding times. I could have stayed at work that day after addressing Wilma. However, I felt like I needed to pick up Zeplyn.

Mrs. Coleman seemed to understand the conversation that we had the day before. I could not understand why the whole issue was blown out of proportion. Not again, I thought. Why would anyone who is defensive, harsh, and has a bad attitude be irresponsive to what I meant? I decided not to call Mrs. Coleman before picking up Zeplyn. I parked down the street since there weren't any spaces in front of the house. I walked to the house and contemplated whether to look into the window. Why would I do that? My mother used to always say that when you look for something, you will usually find it. And I did.

The number of children in Mrs. Coleman's living room had increased to nine. I counted at least nine children before ringing the doorbell. I rang the doorbell. I could see out of the corner of my eye that she looked out of the window first. However, a massive pole on her front porch blocked her from being able to see me. A Federal Express truck was parked out front. She said very loudly, "It's okay; it is just the Fed-Ex man." As she arrived at the door and saw that it was me, her eyes widened, and she said, "Oh, my God." Why do people say that when they are caught by surprise or off guard? That is usually a sign that something is in disarray. Don't they realize that God didn't put them in that compromising position, and had they thought about the consequences of their actions, they probably wouldn't be in that situation?

In my impatience, I said, "No. It is Mrs. Tillman." Since she was standing close to the door, I asked her if I could come in to get Zeplyn. I don't know if she answered the question, but I do know that I was in the middle of her living room. She was standing there with what looked like a three-month-old. Just then, a Hispanic woman came out of the back room holding my child. She was singing a song to him in Spanish, and he had a bottle in his mouth. The problem was that the bottle was not one of mine. I ran over and snatched the bottle from his mouth. I knew it wasn't his. I looked at Mrs. Coleman and asked, "What is going on here, and why does Zeplyn have somebody else's bottle? All of Zeplyn's bottles are clearly labeled with his name typed in large black print." I was livid. I looked down at the child she was holding. He had a bottle in his mouth, and on it, I saw the name ZEPLYN in large black print. After having a few words with Mrs. Coleman, I got my child and left.

PROVIDER #4

Mrs. Moore was the fourth. Again, I couldn't understand why people who appeared to be fine in the beginning later turned out to be unacceptable. I felt like I was being punished. The worst sentiment for a mother is the feeling of helplessness. My husband was a comfort and was the first one to say that maybe these situations were happening for a reason. I believe in divine purpose, but couldn't see what God was showing me.

Mrs. Moore was a reference from a good friend of mine. She had moved from Texas to Virginia three years earlier. Her husband was in the military, and they were stationed in Virginia. She was a petite woman who had a soft-spoken voice. She was welcoming and invited me to have tea with her. She went over the policy manual with me and took me on a tour of her home. She watched two other children. Her only son was eighteen months old. The other child was a two-year-old boy she'd watched since he was four months. I received additional references from her and began checking the names like I did for the three previous childcare providers. The references checked out well. They all said wonderful things about Mrs. Moore. They said she was soft spoken, kind, and patient. They also gave me examples of some of the things they really liked about her. They said she took her job seriously, she was organized and prepared for the children each morning, and she was very inviting and interested in the children and their parents.

One of my questions to Mrs. Moore was if she could have any career what would it be? If this answer was any indication of her dedication, she said, "I would be doing exactly what I am doing now, caring for children." I was glad she felt that way. Zeplyn started there that next week. He smiled when I picked him up and seemed happy to go with Mrs. Moore when I dropped him off. She made me happy because she made Zeplyn happy. That was all I cared about. I thought, why did it take so long to find this woman. AND what purpose did those other people serve? Perhaps one day I would know.

The stockings were by the chimney with care. It was December. Mrs. Moore's house was not only festive, but her attitude was also festive, joyful, and full of laughter. She told me she loved holiday cheer and that her Christmas tree had been up since November. I never knew anyone who put up a Christmas tree right after Thanksgiving. Yes, literally the day after Thanksgiving Mrs. Moore's tree was up. I didn't complain. Her house was cozy, and she brought so much warmth to her place. She treated my son like gold when I was around.

Since I had so many bad experiences, I showed up early to be sure. It was Wednesday morning, and I was early to pick up my son. When I arrived, Mrs. Moore was singing to Zeplyn. She had him wrapped in her arms and held him tightly. I was so happy. I could go to work feeling better than I had in a long time. I could finally try to be productive. Unfortunately, the elation suddenly ended when Mrs. Moore informed me that her husband was being transferred, and she was giving each parent a two-week notice to be prepared. Need I say more? I was on an emotional roller coaster. I was upset and didn't want to find yet another childcare provider. However, after twenty-four hours, I knew that I didn't have any choice.

PROVIDER #5

Mrs. Moore referred her. Her name was Cathy. She had just been getting out of the bed the first and second day I arrived. Although she claimed to be ill over the weekend, I thought to myself, three strikes and you are out. Again, on the third day, she was just getting out of bed. I went to work anyway and started to look at the list of providers. On my way to pick up Zeplyn, I was deciding whether or not to disenroll him from Ms. Cathy. Maybe I could settle this one time. She only got up late three times and was not prepared for my arrival. No way, I thought. I wasn't willing to settle when it came to the welfare of my child. It seemed as if my tolerance level was very low at this point. I was getting tired of dealing with unacceptable performances. It did not take much for me to get fed up.

As I got on the elevator, I pushed the button for the third floor and saw a familiar face. I saw her leaving Ms. Cathy's apartment the day before. Her child had been with Cathy for three months. She looked at me, and we said in unison, "Don't I know you?" We spoke for a few minutes. I told her briefly about the previous childcare providers that I hired. Perhaps the anxiety showed on my face. Whatever it was, she chose to inform me. She asked if she could tell me something. I wanted to say yes, but was afraid of what she might say. She told me she was Eric, the little two-month-old's, mother. "I come to Ms. Cathy every day at 12:30 PM to breastfeed my baby, and your baby has been in the bassinette crying each day. I often think to myself why she wouldn't pick up that little boy. Yesterday it got so bad I couldn't stand it. I asked her why she doesn't pick him up when he cries for so long. Her response was, 'He cries because he is spoiled.'" She said that she was devastated, but decided not to say anything for fear that her child would be treated differently. She said that she was interviewing to find another provider. She ended by saying, "I figure that if she treats your child like that, it won't be long before my child will be treated the same way." I thanked her for being candid and wondered if she would have ever told me had she not seen me that day in the elevator.

I decided to drop by the next day at 12:35 PM. I listened at the door, and sure enough, Zeplyn cried for ten minutes without Cathy saying a word. I rang the doorbell and asked her why she let him cry so long? She answered by saying that he was tired. I told her that we both were well aware of the fact that he just woke up. She was very bold in stating that she doesn't pick up babies just because they cry and that something had to be wrong for her to pick up the child. As she was talking, I went over to pick up Zeplyn, and his diaper was soaked. I looked at her and said, "Something is wrong." I picked up Zeplyn and left.

As I walked down the hallway, I began to think about all of my experiences. I just snatched my child out of the provider's care. Until that very moment, I was not compelled to track and to report her or the other providers I had used to the Division of Licensing. Months later, I was faced with the same drama, and I felt guilty.

CHAPTER 7 PROVIDER #6

This was getting old. I was tired, and if something didn't change for the better really soon, I was going to lose it. I was on the verge of a nervous breakdown. I spent the next three days drafting many letters to my employer. The accounting company where I worked was good to me. It was an African-American–owned company, led by a husband-and-wife team unlike anything I had ever seen before. Mr. Tom was strong and commanded his troops like he was a commander in the army. He was strict and demanded perfection. His wife was kind. She often stood by her man at the expense of their loyal employees who had been there for many years. Although he ran a tight ship, I admired the dedication, determination, and drive of this man.

My mother-in-law came to watch Zeplyn while we attempted to find reliable childcare. We received a call from one of the childcare centers where Zeplyn had been on the waiting list. There was an unexpected opening, and they asked if we would like it. I wanted to visit, and they said that was fine. The next day, I arrived early to find that they had twenty-two children in one very small classroom with one teacher and one assistant. I decided not to take him there because of the high teacher-to-student ratio.

My husband came home excited the next day because he found a childcare provider that he knew I would be happy with. One of his coworkers referred this woman. She had already watched three of his coworkers' children. His persistence forced me to set up an appointment to meet with her.

Ms. Thomas was her name. She was a forty-seven-year-old widower who had two older children in college and a four-year-old granddaughter whom she watched. She was a nice woman, but I wasn't quite settled on the fact that she would be watching my son. I wrestled all night and didn't fall asleep until 3:00 AM. I woke up two hours later and decided to pick up my Bible. I hoped to hear a word from the Lord. I opened the Bible and immediately began reading Philippians 4:10–20. The thirteenth verse stuck out: "I can do all things through Christ who strengthens me." At the time, I assumed the passage was referring to me due to the fact that I had been contemplating whether to hand in my resignation. I knew deep down that it would not be on my time, but it would be on time.

I didn't get more than three hours of sleep that night. We met with Ms. Thomas and spent several hours with her. I decided to leave Zeplyn. I dropped Zeplyn off at 7:30 AM that morning. I walked into Ms. Thomas's home with a bag filled with diapers, wipes, bottles, and extra clothes in my right hand. In my left hand, I had Zeplyn in the car seat. For most of the morning, I felt sick and couldn't get my bearings. For some reason, I felt out of sync. I remember going to work that day and walking into my supervisor's office, wanting to give him the paper that was in my hand. It was a well-written two-week notice of resignation already typed and sealed in an envelope. However, while in his office, I couldn't lift my arm to give him the letter. Why was I feeling so guilty? I was prepared and had practiced my resignation speech more than once. The words just couldn't come out. So I left his office with permission to leave early due to illness. I had the two-week resignation still in my hand.

As I pulled up to Ms. Thomas's house, I noticed a lady leaving her house. Ms. Thomas did not see me coming when she was closing the door. As I put my right hand up to ring the doorbell, I saw an envelope on the porch. I bent down to pick it up. As I stood up, the door opened. The expression on her face was uncanny and all too familiar. I went into the house, and she just stood at the door. I walked into the living room and then into a room where all the noise was coming from. She had a side den off to the left where I left Zeplyn at 7:30 that morning. I arrived at her house at 12:15 PM, and he was still in his car seat. His eyes were closed, and he was sweating. I wanted to take the bag that I had in my hand and haul off and knock her from here to eternity, but instead, I asked her why my child was still in the car seat. She just looked at me. Like the others before her, she could not answer the question. She just stood there looking dumbfounded. I felt HELPLESS, yet again.

PROVIDER #7

There would never have been a seventh except for the fact that this woman had had Zeplyn on a waiting list for three months. She had been interviewed earlier and was hired in the beginning of the process. However, her waiting list was so long at the time that she couldn't enroll Zeplyn.

Helen was her name. She lived three floors downstairs from where we lived. She was an older woman and watched my best friend's son when he was born. She lived in the same building. I was happy and sad when she called. I told her that I had had distressful childcare-provider experiences, and I was deciding what other profession I could pursue at home. I was often depressed and disheartened with the care my son was receiving. She assured me she had been a provider for so many years and truly loved what she was doing. She would not do anything to hurt Zeplyn. The next day, I dropped Zeplyn off at Helen's house. I started taking a real-estate course. Once I passed the test, I would be able to have the freedom to work from home.

The first week went well at Helen's house. Zeplyn reached for her in the morning and seemed happy when I arrived. That next Wednesday, I arrived to pick up Zeplyn, and to my surprise, Helen was in the hallway talking to another person. I immediately went by her. At this point in my experience, my internal feelings took over. I immediately went to her back bedroom. I could feel the anxiety coming over me. He wasn't in the room to the left. I began sweating and went to the room on the right. As I walked into the room, I turned a 360-degree angle and saw Zeplyn in a bassinette. He was semi-asleep. He had a bottle in his mouth, and a ledge protruding from the wall held up the bottle. There was nothing in the bottle, except the plastic bag with no more milk.

If it were not for the person Helen was talking to in the hallway, I don't know what jail I would be in now. I just lost it. I was so upset that I couldn't even speak. I can imagine what temporary insanity is. Something comes over you. I couldn't think about anything except, "What was she thinking?" It really didn't matter what she was thinking. I was out of her apartment and out of the corporate workforce. I had to go. Zeplyn could no longer take such abuse. "What was I thinking all of this time?" I said to myself. I have always been the kind of person who had patience, not like Noah, but patience nonetheless. However, when I have come to the end of my rope, there are never any regrets. I make a habit of not looking back.

So, what was I going to do now? The first thing that came to mind was to hand in that long-awaited resignation that had been hidden in my pocketbook for over one month. However, for the first time in my career, I would not be able to give my employer a two-week notice. The letter therefore read: "Due to extenuating circumstances that are beyond my control, I am resigning my position as staff accountant."

CHOICES

When I first made the decision to quit my job to become a family childcare provider, the main thought that crossed my mind was, I can do this better than all of the other providers I have come in contact with. Not only can I do it better, I must do it better because our children need me to. My only objective was to work hard to make this dream a reality. Remembering the experiences that my child had suffered at the hands of other providers was painful, but it gave me the determination, courage, and diligence to keep trying. If I were to be used by God as a vessel to work to improve the lives of our nation's "little ones," then that was enough for me to feel fulfilled.

Where would I begin? After all, my BA degree was in business administration and political science with a minor in accounting. Although I babysat when I was younger and worked in an after-school program in high school as an assistant teacher, neither experience qualified me to own and operate my own business with children. After completing the twenty-five-hour course, I decided to continue doing research. I believe that when you are working at a job, you should always work toward your next job—meaning, begin with the end in mind. For example, when I began working as an in-home childcare provider, my dream was ultimately to own a childcare center. Therefore, I set up my apartment and prepared all the paperwork as if I were already running a childcare center. I was diligent and patient with children. As a child, doing chores and being responsible proved to be a wonderful foundation for developing a good work ethic.

When the children went home and my child went to sleep, I spent evenings and early morning hours fine-tuning my parent handbooks, announcements, and newsletters. I wrote menus and fed the children meals with nutrition standards required by the United States Department of Agriculture. I designed a curriculum and daily schedules for each age group. I also began to look outside of the home for a larger space.

Before you embark upon this endeavor, be sure that you know why you are doing it. For example, ask yourself if you are attempting to break into this business because you think you will be instantly wealthy or if it is because you sincerely want to improve the quality of life for children and their families? Let me set the record straight—the childcare industry is not the business that will instantly bring you millions of dollars. As a matter of fact, you may never make millions owning and operating your own center. However, if you are in this business for the right reason, and your heart and soul is into it, you will be rich in love, rich in spirit, rich in passion, and rich in being the best that you can be for children—because by being your best, you are able to give your best in return.

I was never guided by the motivation to "get wealthy." Since the beginning, I have been driven by my passion to make this world a better place for children. Therefore, when I began looking outside of the home for a larger space, my objective was to be able to touch the lives of more children. My philosophy was if five children could be affected in a positive way, so could forty-five, one hundred and five, and prayerfully thousands.

I went to City Hall and other property managers, and contacted real-estate agencies to inquire, but nothing seemed to be working out the way I thought it should. Most of the people that I talked to said that space was not available in a particular area of the city or that they didn't want to take on the liability of housing a childcare center or "daycare," as it is often referred to. I also spoke to a licensing specialist and other people who were very discouraging. One lesson I learned as a child was that patience and persistence must take precedence in your life. In addition, what lies behind us and what lies before us are tiny matters compared to what lies within us ~ Oliver Wendell Holmes.

So, when things didn't immediately work out the way I thought it should, I continued to pray and wait for God to lead me. At that point, I didn't do anything but stop and listen. I stopped pounding the pavement. I stopped calling all of the realtors and property managers bugging them day and night, and I stopped harassing the contacts that I had made at City Hall. I began to focus more on right here and now. I strived to make my in-home school the best place it could be. I worked at home for approximately ten months. On October 8, 1993, I received a phone call from the property manager that I had spoken with seven months earlier. He informed me that a childcare center located in an apartment complex had gone out of business after twenty-five years. He also said that he had heard many good things about my in-home childcare. The next words that came out of his mouth changed my life forever: "Would you like to have the center?"

I was informed that the other center lost a child, who was eventually found eight hours later. It was clear at that point that I wanted the location. My family was very instrumental in helping me clean and organize the center. My mother, who was a first-grade teacher for over twenty-five years, was very helpful in setting up the center based on the Division of Licensing requirements. I borrowed $5,000 from my godfather to pay the first and last months' rent. We also used $6,000 from our savings to purchase supplies and equipment. I never attempted to apply for a loan from the bank or SBA. I believed that if it was for me, God would give me a way to work it out. We were blessed to be able to use the existing tables, chairs, and cabinets that the previous center left.

During November through January, I was able to make an appointment with the Division of Licensing to get pointers on how to operate a center. Although the visit was disappointing, it turned out to be one of the best things that ever happened. I spoke to the licensing specialist about my plans. Then she told me that many people come to her also wanting to open a center. However, she discourages most of them, and I wouldn't be any different. She commented that she had two centers in the past that went out of business. She stated it was extremely difficult to own and operate a childcare center, and it was not the get-rich scheme that many people thought it was. In fact, she flat out said that I could not do it. My background was not in early childhood education, and therefore, I had no expertise for the childcare industry. In addition, she contended that people go to school for years and still are not successful.

What she didn't know about me was that my idea of success was not "to get rich." It was working smart, being the best person that I could be, and living each day like it was the first day of my life. In addition, anyone who knows me knows that I welcome a challenge. As I sat there listening to her say that I couldn't do it, I remembered reading the book *The Little Engine That Could* to my son the night before. That children's book is a wonderful tool for teaching children and adults about courage and self-determination. I did not leave her office as she had hoped, feeling defeated and in despair. I left with faith knowing that with God all things are possible. As I walked out of the door into the parking lot, I began chanting, "I think I can! I think I can! I think I can! … I know I can!"

# ARE YOU READY?

Before we talk about how to open a quality childcare center, we first need to decide whether or not you need to be in the field of early childhood education. Needing to be in this field has less to do with your education, credentials, or your love for children. It has more to do with your having the qualities to endure. The early childhood education field does not need just another mediocre "daycare," a place to babysit or house children. It needs exceptional people with exceptional ideas to make exceptional things happen. It needs centers that go beyond their greatest imaginations to bring forth and create something that will last and be an inspiration to children and families. In effect, you must be willing to change lives in a positive way. In order to do this, you need to be equipped with what I coin the 3 Ps: passion, patience, and persistence. Passion is defined as a strong emotion. Being passionate about your calling to make a difference in the lives of children is what is important, as is having a strong conviction to do whatever you can to make certain that the lives of children are enriched. Passion means that you would work even if you never earned a penny. Passion is love—love for what you are doing.

Patience with the children is essential to operating your own childcare center. It is also imperative that you are patient with yourself. Don't rush things into fruition. Take your time, organize yourself, and patiently wait for it to happen.

Persistence. I don't know anyone who ever owned or operated a center who wasn't persistent. You must have the tenacity and wherewithal to continue in spite of the difficulties, in spite of people telling you it can't be done, and sometimes in spite of your own insecurities. If it means that much to you, you will be like the Little Engine That Could and also say, "I think I can. I think I can."

Once you have determined that this is your calling and you have the 3 Ps, you must be willing to do what I have coined the 3 Ws: work hard, work long, and work out.

There is a misconception about working hard. To work hard doesn't always mean working until you get tired or burnt out. Working hard means that you work toward making the best decisions and the most precise calculations when you are at your best. Working long can mean and most often means that you will not be working 9:00 AM–5:00 PM. There will be no time clock for you to use to check in and out. Your clock is your conscience. Your conscience must be willing and able to rise early and retire late. You are more than the hours of operation. You are evenings and weekends and holidays. You are also responsible for getting at least eight hours of sleep and a nap. You and your business will suffer without sufficient downtime.

Work out. One of the biggest mistakes you can make is to neglect your mind and body. You have an obligation to everyone to take care of yourself (without feeling guilty). Take the time to work out at a minimum of three times per week and eat well-balanced meals and snacks. *"Remember that things which matter the most must never be at the mercy of things which matter least"* ~ Goethe. You are what matters the most. Take time out to be good to you!

 PLANNING

The old saying is true: ***"People don't plan to fail; they just fail to plan."*** Let's face it; you don't get into your car, drive to the airport, and then decide on where you are going. Without a plan in place, you will aimlessly be on a journey that is sure to end in disaster. A plan is your purpose and your priority. When I started writing a plan, I began with a statement of purpose, or a mission statement. The mission statement should tell what the function or purpose of the business is. It should give an overview of what people will be expected to find if and when they become your clients. For example, the Happy Home mission statement is geared toward educating and guiding children between the ages of one and five years old. We focus on cultivating self-esteem, providing self-discipline, social relations, and fostering physical and mental growth. We believe that children learn by recognizing that they are unique and special with individual physical, social, emotional, and intellectual needs and abilities. Our child-centered program emphasizes the development of positive self-image and the fulfillment of each child's potential.

Once you have a precise mission in place, you can begin working on developing more details of your business plan. First, give a description of the business, and if you know where the location will be, include that as well. Take time to scope out your competition. Get a list of other childcare centers within a ten-mile radius. Visit those schools and get an idea of how their operation runs in terms of operating policies and procedures. This is important because it will not only help you develop your own center, it will also help you add services that other centers do not provide. Overall, you should identify the strengths and weaknesses of your competitors.

For example, if most of the nearby centers open at 7:00 AM, you may want to open your center at 6:00 AM or 6:30 AM. The extra time that parents have to get to work might just make the difference between choosing your center and someone else's. In other words, find ways to make your home-care environment or center special. You must also determine what market you intend to serve, its size, and your anticipated share of the market. Include an explanation as to why you can serve the market better than your competitors.

Your plan should also discuss how you would envision your center to be set up.

There are four ways you can organize your new business: sole proprietorship, partnership, corporation, and limited liability company. There are advantages and disadvantages of forming your business in each of these ways. Decide what is best for you. Finding a good lawyer and accountant to retain in the beginning will be the smartest thing that you can ever do. They can assist you in outlining the benefits of your setup. Even if you decide to begin at home as a childcare provider, start thinking about these things. It will make a difference in the long run.

LICENSING REQUIREMENTS

The licensing requirements for an in-home facility and a center are different. You need to obtain a family childcare provider's certificate for an in-home center. The process varies depending upon location. Check with your local Department of Social Services for specific application requirements. The requirements in the City of Alexandria included the completion of a twenty-five-hour provider course. There was an application, reference checks, criminal background checks, and a home visit from the social worker in order to ensure that your home was considered safe for children. The completion of the twenty-five-hour course (now thirty-five hours) made me agency approved and qualified me to become a family childcare provider. The course was very short and not difficult to complete.

While I was taking the course, I learned about policies and procedures for running an in-home childcare. I found the health and safety guidelines and the procedures of how to make your home childproof to be very beneficial. I couldn't believe how easy it was to become a provider. I only needed to complete some paperwork to become registered. I also had to successfully complete the twenty-five-hour course to become agency approved.

Childcare centers are regulated by states, which provide minimum standards for owning and operating a childcare program. Remember that the standards are just the "minimum." You need to go beyond what is required in order to operate a quality childcare center.

Next we decided upon a name for my business and registered the name at the local courthouse. My husband actually came up with the name Happy Home Child Learning Center. He said that he chose the word *HAPPY* because it was how he wanted me to feel when Zeplyn was in childcare. He said that he chose the word *HOME* because I made our house into a home, which was a loving and desirable place to be. Thus, the name HAPPY HOME.

"Child Learning Center" was chosen because I always felt that the word *daycare* did not truly exemplify what teachers and providers do each and every day.

Once I registered the name with the court, I visited City Hall for a business license and the Code enforcement for a certificate of occupancy. If the property that you plan to purchase is already a childcare center, you may only need a change of ownership. However, if it is being used differently, you may need to apply for a special use permit. A special use permit takes longer to get, depending on the city calendar zoning office for approval.

DEVELOPING POLICIES BASED ON REQUIREMENTS

When formulating a policies and procedures manual, there are several elements that are mandatory and are a requirement of the Division of Licensing. Your parent handbook should contain all of the rules and regulations listed in Appendix A. Each state will have its own Division of Licensing minimum standards book, so be sure to follow those guidelines. It is important that you put a tremendous amount of time and effort into writing a parent handbook that is informative and parent friendly. Below are some elements that should be included in the parent handbook.

Begin with a welcome statement. I wanted parents to know and understand the impact that home and family have on a child's development. A child's first teacher is his or her parents. I also wanted parents to know that we solicit their cooperation and support to make this joint effort between home, workplace, and school a happy and meaningful experience for all. Our school takes the first step in supporting and caring for their children. We hope that they will join us in our efforts.

After completing the parent handbook, I began to interview parents. The number of parents who did their homework impressed me. They came with many questions and asked me how I would handle a variety of issues. Many were first-time parents and had various questions regarding potty training, stages of development, and discipline issues.

I continued to educate myself. I enrolled in a local community college and began taking courses in early childhood development. I learned about the philosophers and various stages of development for young children. I continued my studies for one year and took over five introductory courses. I took courses in intro to early childhood education, creative activities, nutrition, health and safety, and guiding behavior. I also received my license from the Northern Virginia Food Handling Company.

STAFFING

When I began writing my employee handbook, I didn't have employees. However, I have always realized that the staff was the most important aspect of any business. A teacher's inner being is much more important than the subject or information that he or she is teaching. I thought a lot about my fifth-grade teacher, Ms. Neals, who always believed in her students, particularly those students no one else believed in. She went that extra mile to make sure that she wouldn't lose many of those ten-year-old children. She believed in them, and they started to believe in themselves. I kept her in mind as I organized the employee handbook.

I wanted to be sure that my objectives were clearly formatted. One of my objectives was to provide compensation that was competitive and internally equitable. I also wanted to reward employees based on their contribution to the company's success; to maintain a safe, healthy, and productive work environment; to provide equal opportunity to all employees and all applicants; to avoid the fact or perception of unfair advantage and to recognize and enforce the rights of all employees to work in an environment that is free of harassment and discrimination based on age, race, color, national origin, sex, religion, or veteran or handicapped status; and to maintain and enhance a quality workforce through the careful selection, retention, motivation, and recognition of qualified individuals that meets and/or exceeds the requirements of the Department of Licensing.

I wanted to ensure and promote the highest ethical standards for the employees, managers, and the company. I must say that finding and retaining reliable staff has always been the most challenging aspect of being an owner. It is important to design an employee manual that discusses topics that are important to you. Remember that staff, as well as parents, will refer back to the manuals. Therefore, be sure that whatever you put in your manual will be crucial to making your business the best place to be. Appendix B includes a sample employee handbook.

When looking for prospective teachers, I placed many ads in local newspapers. I also made attractive flyers and distributed them to local colleges and universities.

I included our phone number so that I could get an idea of how they sounded on the phone. I have the prospective employee work with me for a day in order to determine how he or she interacts with children and adults. By that time, I can usually determine whether he or she is a good match.

CURRICULUM
DEVELOPMENT

The interaction between the adult and the child for Vygotsky is like a dance—the child leads and the adult follows, always closely in tune with the child's actions.

Now that I had more than five children, I had to find something to keep them occupied other than the television and games. I never wanted to make the mistakes that I had seen from other providers. Several didn't mind children watching TV for most of the day, followed by a nap, a change of diapers, and more TV. Unfortunately, that was their routine, and I wanted more for the children in my care.

We started each day with a morning prayer or a positive affirmation, a concept that is still prominent in my centers. We then continued with the Happy Home motto. Since I had five children varying in ages, the attempt to design a challenging yet stimulating curriculum was demanding. I began by researching various curriculums; unfortunately, none of them were perfect. My main objective was to first devise goals and objectives for the children. I wanted a curriculum that would meet the individual needs of the young child, whereby there was time and opportunity in a planned educational environment for the social, intellectual, emotional, and physical growth of the child at his or her own rate of development.

Some of the objectives were to extend an integrated day to encompass the whole life of the child during the early formative years of exploration and discovery.

♦ To recognize the child as a creative individual having certain innate tendencies, potentialities, and traits, and also to accept him or her as a member of society having certain rights and privileges, duties, and responsibilities.

- ♦ To give a child ample opportunity to work and play independently, to learn, and to live effectively with himself and others. To develop a sense of identity, to experience many chances for success, and to enrich and broaden intellectual, social, and physical development.

- ♦ To provide free choices, "I am special" time, "circle" time, and interaction with friends that give the child opportunities to grow in the early years.

- ♦ To provide the child in the center with rich experiences to promote the whole child.

- ♦ To provide early learning experiences for each and every individual.

- ♦ To provide experiences in which a child can work individually and/or within a group.

- ♦ To provide experiences that enrich and promote good morals and values.

The preschool curriculum should provide a challenging yet enjoyable experience for children. At every level of development, children follow a flexible curriculum, mastering skills in the core areas of social, emotional, and language development. We recognize the physical, socio-emotional, and intellectual uniqueness of each child and strive to provide for his or her special needs and abilities. We encourage children to think critically and to develop the skills, curiosity, self-confidence, and discipline necessary to learn throughout life.

In preschools, worthwhile learning experiences and desirable development does not just "happen." A teacher must make them happen. Good learning requires that a teacher knows the kind of educational experiences that young children need. This is especially true today when children need special skills to cope with rapid changes in our society. That is one of the main reasons why I went back to school to obtain my master's degree in early childhood special education.

When designing your preschool curriculum, remember that despite popular opinion, children learn through play. At Happy Home we don't call it "play"; we refer to it as "work." Children are given the opportunity to work throughout the day in several areas of interest. The art center, for example, is designated to be a busy production center. Ideally, it should have a water source. The storage space should allow children to find a variety of materials easily accessible, in labeled tubs. Materials such as crayons and scissors are organized so that the children can use and replace them. Playing is an important aspect in children's development. All representational play creates imaginary situations that permit the child to grapple with unrealizable desires. Fantasy play makes its appearance at a time when children must learn to postpone the gratification of impulses and accept the fact that certain desires will remain unsatisfied. Make-believe play therefore supports the emergence of two complementary capacities.

BLOCK CENTER

This should be in a construction area designed for movement and large materials. It should have a well-defined space with open-style bookcases for storage and low nap carpet on the floor.

BOOK CENTER

This should be designated to be a comfortable space where children relax, enjoy, and explore books. Our main objective is to make the book center so appealing that the interest in books creates a whole new world for children. Make sure to have hard books accessible to young children as well as big books. Include some of the classics like *Goodnight Moon*, *The Little Engine That Could*, and *The Growing Tree*. Lists of books to include in the library are located in the index at the back of this book.

LISTENING CENTER

Here, children are able to listen to a story while they follow the printed version in the book, thus, reinforcing the concept of language, both oral and written. This is a wonderful tool for improving comprehension skills.

WOODWORKING CENTER

Give children an opportunity to work with tools and materials to create their own designs. You may want to use this with the four- and five-year-old classes only. Make sure that children who work with wood have good motor skills.

DRAMATIC PLAY CENTER

This allows children to re-create the social roles they see in their everyday lives. The setup of the center is designed to encourage children to explore the roles of parents, children, and workers. Communicating with other children is a key skill we see at the center.

MANIPULATIVE CENTER (TABLE TOYS)

This center provides children with interesting materials to use for exploration. Research shows that exploration time is beneficial in supporting children's understanding in mathematical, logical, and critical thinking.

COMPUTER CENTER

The computer station is designed to help children focus on auditory skills and fine motor skills.

With these centers in place, a typical day for a one- through five-year-old would be as shown in Figure 2–4.

When choosing themes, observe children throughout the day to determine what they are interested in. Then you can plan a well-designed curriculum for them based on their needs and wants. This is one reason why preplanned curriculums are not very popular at Happy Home. They tend to allow for more teacher preparation and less child-oriented preparation.

UNITS AND THEMES

The curriculum for our children is developed around the use of "themes." Some of these themes may include, but are not limited to, the following:

- Buildings
- Children around the world
- Colors and shapes
- Community workers
- Dinosaurs
- Families
- Farm animals
- Friends
- Fire prevention
- Food and nutrition
- Health and safety
- Holidays and seasons
- House pets
- I am special
- Plant life and gardening
- The five senses
- Space and the solar system
- Transportation
- Weather
- Zoo animals

BUSY BEES
DAILY SCHEDULE
(1-2 1/2 YRS. OLD)

7:00 a.m. - 8:00 a.m.	Self Initiated play (centers) breakfast
8:00 a.m. -	Children separate into individual groups
8:30 a.m. -	Diapers
9:00 a.m. - 9:15 a.m.	Circle Time (songs, theme)
9:15 a.m. - 9:30 a.m.	Restroom
9:30 a.m. - 10:00 a.m.	Outdoors (gross motor skills)
10:00 a.m. - 10:20 a.m.	Wash Hands & Snack
10:20 a.m. - 10:30 a.m.	Diapers/potty
10:30 a.m. - 11:00 a.m.	Morning Projects, Art Activities (Center Time)
11:00 a.m. - 11:05 a.m.	Wash hands
11:05 a.m. - 11:30 a.m.	Stories, puppet shows, language, felt board
11:30 a.m. - 12:00 p.m.	Lunch
12:00 p.m. - 12:30 p.m.	Restroom, prepare for naps
12:30 p.m. - 2:30 p.m.	Naptime
2:30 p.m. - 3:15 p.m.	Diaper changing, hands, face, shoes, etc.
3:15 p.m. - 3:30 p.m.	Afternoon snack
3:30 p.m. - 4:00 p.m.	Outdoors (gross motor skills)
4:00 p.m. - 4:30 p.m.	Wash Hands & Center based activities
4:30 p.m. - 5:00 p.m.	Afternoon Projects
5:00 p.m. - 6:00 p.m.	Short stories & manipulative

Figure 1. Sample Daily Schedule for 1–2½-Year-Olds.

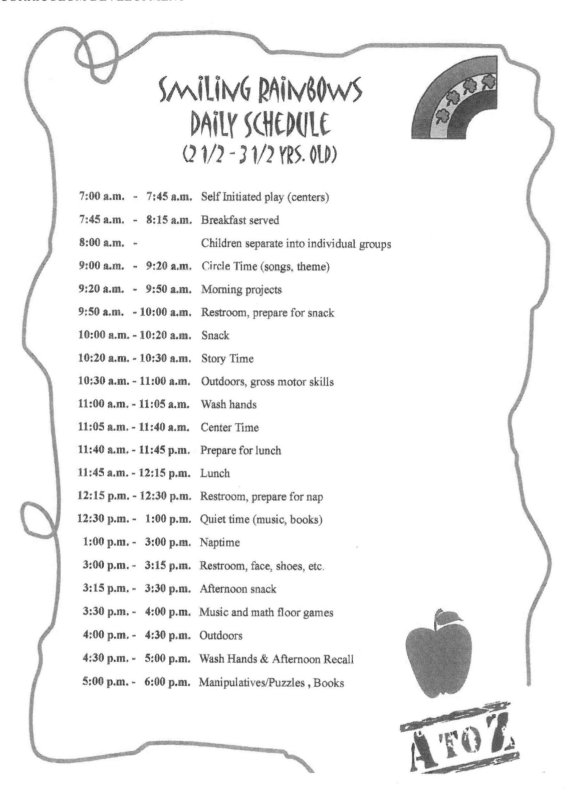

SMILING RAINBOWS DAILY SCHEDULE
(2 1/2 - 3 1/2 YRS. OLD)

7:00 a.m. - 7:45 a.m.	Self Initiated play (centers)
7:45 a.m. - 8:15 a.m.	Breakfast served
8:00 a.m. -	Children separate into individual groups
9:00 a.m. - 9:20 a.m.	Circle Time (songs, theme)
9:20 a.m. - 9:50 a.m.	Morning projects
9:50 a.m. - 10:00 a.m.	Restroom, prepare for snack
10:00 a.m. - 10:20 a.m.	Snack
10:20 a.m. - 10:30 a.m.	Story Time
10:30 a.m. - 11:00 a.m.	Outdoors, gross motor skills
11:00 a.m. - 11:05 a.m.	Wash hands
11:05 a.m. - 11:40 a.m.	Center Time
11:40 a.m. - 11:45 p.m.	Prepare for lunch
11:45 a.m. - 12:15 p.m.	Lunch
12:15 p.m. - 12:30 p.m.	Restroom, prepare for nap
12:30 p.m. - 1:00 p.m.	Quiet time (music, books)
1:00 p.m. - 3:00 p.m.	Naptime
3:00 p.m. - 3:15 p.m.	Restroom, face, shoes, etc.
3:15 p.m. - 3:30 p.m.	Afternoon snack
3:30 p.m. - 4:00 p.m.	Music and math floor games
4:00 p.m. - 4:30 p.m.	Outdoors
4:30 p.m. - 5:00 p.m.	Wash Hands & Afternoon Recall
5:00 p.m. - 6:00 p.m.	Manipulatives/Puzzles , Books

Figure 2. Sample Daily Schedule for 2 ½–3 ½-Year-Olds.

SMALL WONDERS DAILY SCHEDULE
(3 - 4 YRS. OLD)

7:00 a.m.	– 7:45 a.m.	Self Initiated play (centers)
7:45 a.m.	– 8:15 a.m.	Breakfast served
8:00 a.m.	–	Children separate into individual groups
9:00 a.m.	– 9:20 a.m.	Circle Time (songs, theme)
9:20 a.m.	– 9:50 a.m.	Morning projects
9:50 a.m.	– 10:00 a.m.	Restroom, prepare for snack
10:00 a.m.	– 10:20 a.m.	Snack
10:20 a.m.	– 11:00 a.m.	Center Time
11:00 a.m.	– 11:30 a.m.	Outdoors, gross motor skills
11:30 a.m.	– 11:35 a.m.	Wash hands
11:35 a.m.	– 11:55 a.m.	Language/Math Activities
11:55 a.m.	– 12:00 p.m.	Prepare for lunch
12:00 a.m.	– 12:30 p.m.	Lunch
12:30 p.m.	– 1:00 p.m.	Quiet time (music, books)
1:00 p.m.	– 3:00 p.m.	Naptime
3:00 p.m.	– 3:15 p.m.	Restroom, face, shoes, etc.
3:15 p.m.	– 3:30 p.m.	Afternoon snack
3:30 p.m.	– 4:00 p.m.	Circle Time Afternoon Recall
4:00 p.m.	– 4:30 p.m.	Language Activities, music and floor puzzles
4:30 p.m.	– 5:00 p.m.	Outdoors
5:00 p.m.	– 6:00 p.m.	Wash Hands Manipulatives/Puzzles , Books

Figure 3. Sample Daily Schedule for 3–4-Year-Olds.

SHINING STARS DAILY SCHEDULE (4-5 YRS. OLD)

7:00 a.m. - 7:45 a.m.	Self Initiated play (centers)
7:45 a.m. - 8:15 a.m.	Breakfast
8:00 a.m. -	Children separate into individual groups
9:00 a.m. - 9:20 a.m.	Circle Time (songs, theme)
9:20 a.m. - 9:50 a.m.	Language and fine motor skills
9:50 a.m. - 10:00 a.m.	Restroom, prepare for snack
10:00 a.m. - 10:20 a.m.	Snack
10:20 a.m. - 10:30 a.m.	Story time
10:30 a.m. - 11:00 a.m.	Centers based activities
11:00 a.m. - 11:25 a.m.	Science activity hands of discovery
11:25 a.m. - 11:30 a.m.	Tidy up time and prep for gross motor
11:30 a.m. - 11:55 p.m.	Outdoors
11:55 p.m. - 12:00 p.m.	Prepare for lunch
12:00 p.m. - 12:30 p.m.	Lunch
12:30 p.m. - 12:40 p.m.	Restroom, prepare for naps
12:40 p.m. - 1:00 p.m.	Quiet time (Music)
1:00 p.m. - 3:00 p.m.	Naptime
3:00 p.m. - 3:15 p.m.	Restroom, face, shoes, etc.
3:15 p.m. - 3:30 p.m.	Afternoon snack
3:30 p.m. - 4:00 p.m.	Art project (clay, dough)
4:00 p.m. - 4:30 p.m.	Music or math and language activity
4:30 p.m. - 5:00 p.m.	Language, puzzles and team games
5:00 p.m. - 5:30 p.m.	Outdoors
5:30 p.m. - 5:40 p.m.	Restroom (wash hands and face)
5:40 p.m. - 6:00 p.m.	Short stories and math manipulatives

Figure 4. Sample Daily Schedule for 4–5-Year-Olds.

ROOM ARRANGEMENT AND DESIGN

Many administrators often overlook the importance of designing a room that is appropriate to early childhood education. Each piece of equipment and its location in the classroom is extremely important to the management of that classroom. I have learned how crucial it is to place the book center in an area where other quiet centers are present.

For example, the listening center, writing center, and book center can be in an area together to meet the needs of children. Music and movement, the block area, and the housekeeping area can be in close proximity to each other. It makes a difference where the tables, cabinets, and desks are placed. See Figure 5–10 for room diagrams and center elements.

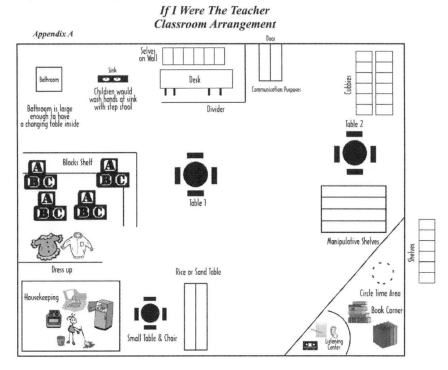

Figure 5. Example of a Room Arrangement.

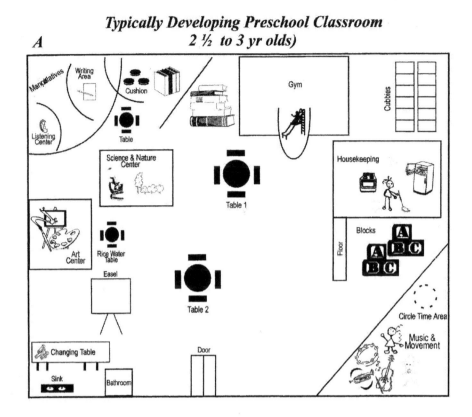

Figure 6. Sample Room Arrangement for 2 ½- to 3-Year-Old Classroom.

The art center is used by the children as a creative mechanism to express themselves. The centers are well-stocked with a variety of paper, markers, crayons, colored pencils, alphabet stamps, envelopes, scissors, and other writing utensils.

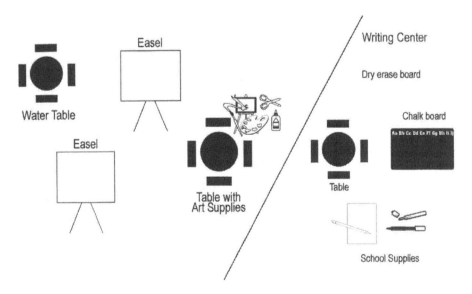

Figure 7. Promoting Literacy in the Art Center.

The reading center is equipped with a wide variety of books, including nursery rhyme books, song picture books, books with repetitive patterns, variously shaped books, chunky board books, vinyl books, peek-a-boo books, books with textures, and big books (e.g., *Old MacDonald, Over in the Meadow,* and *Wheels on the Bus*).

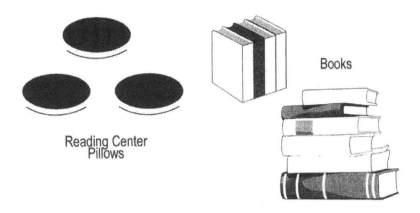

Figure 8. Promoting Literacy in the Reading Center.

The listening center provides cassette tapes, tape recorders, and headphones. It is an extension of facilitating and encouraging early writing behaviors. The center is used in collaboration with books and the writing center to promote the discussion of various books and other topics.

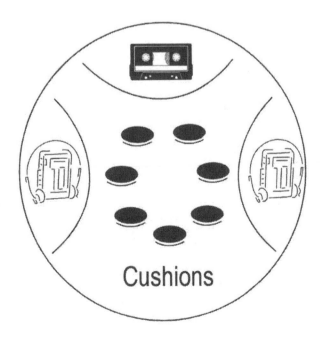

Figure 9. Promoting Literacy in the Listening Center.

The housekeeping center is an invitation to communicate. This center should be clean, cozy, and realistic in environmental settings. Extension and open-ended questions and turn-taking should be used to facilitate speech.

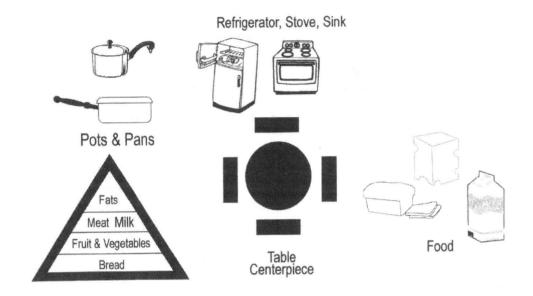

Figure 10. Promoting Literacy in the Housekeeping Center.

The block area is used to enhance and stimulate language development. The area should be stocked with many blocks of different sizes and shapes.

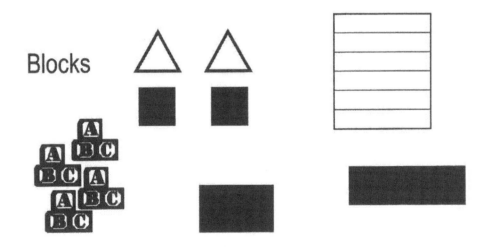

Figure 11. Promoting Literacy in the Block Area.

Children love movement. It is stimulating and fascinating for them to move their bodies to movement. Literacy is promoted because children communicate and talk about how their bodies are changing through movement.

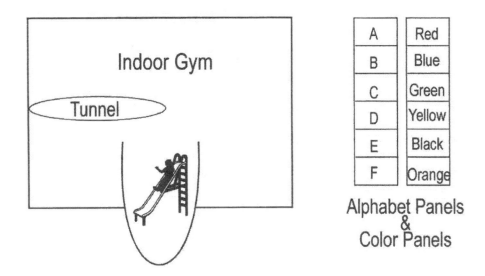

Figure 12. Promoting Literacy Through Gross Motor Development.

When children move to music, sing, and dance, all forms of communication exist. Children sing and dance to music. They play instruments and communicate their actions.

Figure 13. Promoting Literacy in the Music Center.

 FOOD AND NUTRITION

Food and nutrition has always been one of the most important concerns for me as an administrator. Personally, I have been dedicated to ensuring that children have the proper diet and nutrition. Fast foods are fine once or twice a month, but they should never be substituted for healthy daily nutrition. In the beginning, I cooked breakfast and lunch, and dinner for children who were not picked up until after 5:30 PM. I also read various books on creative, nutritious snacks and made every effort to provide children with them.

I applied to the United States Department of Agriculture Food and Nutrition Service after opening the center. They were a great resource in providing me with materials and information on what consisted of a healthy snack. Figure 14 is a sample list of daily morning and afternoon snacks.

WEEK 1

Happy Home Child Learning Center

Week of: _____

MENU

Monday

Breakfast:
Cheerios.................... 1 cup
Milk............................ 3/4 cup
Orange Juice............. 1/2 cup

AM Snack:
Goldfish Crackers (1 oz.)....... 1/4 cup
Apples............................. 1/2 cup

PM Snack:
Saltine Crackers................. 3 each
Oranges............................1 slice

Tuesday

Breakfast:
Corn Flakes.............. 1 cup
Milk.......................... 3/4 cup
Oranges.................... 2 slices

AM Snack:
Fruit Cocktail.............. 1 cup
Ritz Cracker.............. 4 each
100% Apple Juice.........1/2 cup

PM Snack:
Vanilla Wafers........... 2 each
Applesauce............... 1/2 cup

Wednesday

Breakfast:
Cheerios.................... 1 cup
Milk.......................... 3/4 cup
Apple juice .... 1/2 cup

AM Snack:
Ritz Crackers (1/2 oz.)... 4 each
American Cheese......... 1 slice

PM Snack:
American Cheese........... 1 slice
Carrot Sticks.............. 1/2 cup
100% Apple Juice......... 1/2 cup

Thursday

Breakfast:
Mini Bagels.............. 1 each
Milk......................... 3/4 cup
Oranges.................. 1 slice

AM Snack:
Saltine Crackers......... 4 crackers
American Cheese........ 1 slice

PM Snack:
Cheese Crackers......... 2 each
Applesauce.............. 1/2 cup

Friday

Breakfast:
Rice Krispies.............. 1 cup
Milk......................... 3/4 cup
Apples .... 1/2 slice

AM Snack:
Ritz Crackers............. 4 each
100% Apple Juice......... 1/2 cup

PM Snack:
Granola Bar................. 1 each
Oranges.................... 1 slice

Figure 14. Sample List of Daily Morning and Afternoon Snacks.

DEVELOPING A FINANCIAL PLAN

Developing a financial management plan is paramount to the success of any business. Success of your childcare business depends upon a sound budget and a plan that provides a realistic projection of actual estimated expenses and income. Preparing a start-up budget and an operating budget will let you know how much you will spend (now and later) and where the money will come from to start and operate your center. Most importantly, these budgets will indicate whether your projected income will meet your expenses.

The first step in building a sound financial plan is developing a start-up budget. This will usually include one-time costs such as major equipment, renovations, down payments, business insurance, and retaining a good lawyer and accountant. Additionally, your start-up budget should include at least 60 percent to 90 percent of the days' operating costs. In estimating your costs, find out the costs of other childcare centers. For example, ask what their planned and unplanned expenses were to begin and where they have been over the past three years. Make sure that you figure in the current inflation rate. The chart below will help you identify the items to include in your start-up budget.

Start-up Budget

Expenses

Personnel (cost prior to opening)

Down payment or purchase of building

Remodeling costs

Rent

Utilities

Criminal Record Checks

Social Services Child Protective Service background check

Salaries and benefits

Food (first 3 months)

Telephone

Temporary Help

Contractor

Architect

Supplies

Program

Office

Paper products (toilet paper and cleaning supplies)

Legal and Professional Fees

License and Permits

Business insurance

Liability

Workers Compensation

Consultants

Attorney

Advertising and Publications

Professional fees

Seminars & Conferences

Accreditation

Recruitment

Equipment

Playgroup

Telephone

Program & Office

Installation and Delivery Fees

DEVELOPING A MARKETING PLAN

How you market your center can make a difference in its success and failure. Like other businesses, a childcare center provides a service that consumers want and are willing to purchase. Therefore, you will have to sell your service to the consumers (parents). Your marketing plan can help you achieve this goal.

Knowing your customer is the key to successfully marketing your center. The more you know about parents' expectations, the easier it will be to develop a program that meets their needs and the children's needs. The data collected while assessing your community's needs will help you do this. Also, develop a list of questions to help you identify what the parents will likely need, want, and expect of your center. Use the data collected in your initial assessment and the survey to help answer those questions.

Many first-time business owners think that simply placing an advertisement in the local newspaper or airing a commercial on a local radio or television station will make customers flock to purchase their product or service. This may be true to a certain extent, but hundreds, even thousands, of other possible customers may never hear of your business. Think of the money you will lose, simply because you didn't develop an adequate marketing program.

There are certain factors you should consider when developing your marketing strategy. These are called the Five Ps of Marketing.

1. **Product/service**—The description of the product or service.

2. **Price**—An amount competitive within the market area.

3. **Place**—The description of the location, including its advantages, such as adequate parking, good street lighting, easy access.

4. **Promotion**—The method of advertising or highlighting your business.

5. **Persuasion**—The ability to sell your services and the business to the surrounding community.

Each factor requires an investment in dollars, time, and effort, but the reward is worth it. Devise a plan that uses advertising and networking (word-of-mouth advertising) to promote your center. Develop sharp, descriptive copy to clearly identify the services provided by your center, the price of those services, and the center's location. Use catchy phrases to arouse the interest of your readers, listeners, or viewers. Remember, the more care and attention you devote to your marketing program, the more successful your center will be.

No matter what advertising media you use, you will spend money. So, allow for advertising expenses in your budget. There are many ways to advertise your center, but keep in mind that advertising costs vary with the medium used. Newspaper advertisements and radio and television commercials are the most expensive means of advertising. If you can afford to use one of these media, talk to an advertising agency before making a final decision. Once you have decided on the medium, get the agency to help you design your advertisement or create a commercial.

Whatever advertising media you use, be sure to include the following information:

◆ Name, address, and telephone number of the center

◆ Ages of children who will be accepted

◆ Hours the center will be open

◆ Fees charged

◆ A description of the program and the qualifications of the staff

◆ Person(s) to contact for more information

◆ Date you plan to open

Start advertising your center at least three months before you open for business. Make sure your advertisements are consistent with the image you are trying to project. Again, it never hurts to meet your competition head on. Look at your competitors. In what sections do they advertise? What size advertisements do they use?

INEXPENSIVE ADVERTISING TECHNIQUES

If you do not have the money to advertise by radio, television, or newspaper, don't be discouraged. There are other inexpensive yet effective alternatives. A brief description of each follows.

FLIERS AND BROCHURES

One inexpensive way to advertise is to post fliers in public buildings, such as shopping centers, markets, Laundromats, restaurants, and community centers. In the beginning, I placed fliers wherever I thought parents and children would be. Distributing brochures is another good way to advertise. Take brochures or fliers to employment offices, libraries, schools, personnel offices of businesses and industries, government agencies, hospitals, union headquarters or shops, women's groups, colleges and universities, church groups, and parent-teacher associations.

To develop effective brochures and fliers, study written advertisements in the newspapers and magazines, ask yourself which advertisements appeal to you and why, and try to develop similar ones. If you know people in advertising or public relations, ask them to help you design your brochures and fliers to avoid the cost of professional help.

BUSINESS CARDS

Business cards are an excellent, inexpensive way to advertise. Have business cards printed in bulks of 1,000. Include your name, address, and telephone number; the hours of your center; and the ages of the children you'll care for. Ask parents, friends, and relatives to pass them out to interested people at work. Take them along to pass out when you take the children on a field trip or a walk in the neighborhood. Anyone who works with families may be able to make referrals to you—ministers or rabbis, school staff, pediatricians, parent groups, and business or civic organizations. Provide them with business cards, fliers, or brochures on your center so they can knowledgeably talk to prospective clients.

REFERRAL AGENCIES

The number of childcare referral agencies is growing. When you are licensed or registered, you may be eligible to be listed for referrals by the licensing office and other referral agencies in your community. Check the National Directory of Child Care Information and Referral Agencies for the agency nearest you.

NETWORKING

Perhaps one of the best ways to market your center is through networking. Since most parents choose their child's caregiver by word of mouth, talk about yourself and your program to people who might have the opportunity to recommend you. Volunteer to speak to local civic and church groups and the PTA. Networking adds credibility to your service that advertising can't. This is primarily because advertisements are designed to convince people to purchase a certain product or service at any cost, while word-of-mouth referrals are based on an individual's satisfaction with a product or service. Since most people value their families' and friends' judgment more than an advertisement, they will more likely choose your center if it is so recommended.

Remember, advertising by way of word of mouth depends on the quality of your program. If parents are pleased with the way their children are thriving at your center, they will tell their friends. Good providers in clean, safe, and appealing centers are in high demand almost everywhere.

YELLOW PAGES

Directory advertising is completely different from other forms of advertising. It is for people who are ready to buy. See how other quality childcare centers are listed and attempt to be more appealing. Include as much information as possible in your directory advertisement because people frequently make decisions based on the information in the directories.

As with any print media, be sure your entire market is covered by the intended directory with minimal waste.

CLASSIFIED ADS

Place an advertisement in the classified section of your local newspaper. Announce your opening in the business section and the dates and times of your open house, since many people read the business and classified sections of the newspaper during their commute to and from work. Placing an advertisement in these sections can increase your clientele base.

KNOW THE COMPETITION

A cardinal rule of effective marketing is to know your competitors. Assess their operations and find a way to beat them. Many entrepreneurs mistakenly believe that their competitors consist solely of firms that offer similar services or products in the same geographic area. However, they may also include any business vying for the same clients.

Your estimate of competitors should include all those who offer related services. They may be in the same geographic area or another area that is accessible to your clients. To determine the compositeness of your market, find out:

- What businesses offer childcare service.
- Who your major competitors are, both direct and indirect (e.g., childcare centers accessible to your clientele).
- How long your competitors have been in business.
- How your center will benefit the clients more than competitors' centers.
- If there is a need for additional centers in your area or in an area that is easily accessible.
- How competitors' centers are similar to or different from yours.
- What your competitors' strengths and weaknesses are.
- How competitors' businesses are faring.
- How competitors will act when you enter the market.
- What competitors' managerial abilities, financial situations, facilities' reputations, etc. are.

Financial institutions and investors often place heavy emphasis on potential competition when deciding whether to fund a new business. If you apply for a loan to finance your center, it is good to know as much as possible about your competitors.

Market research consultants are professionals who complete market survey reports. They can also help you develop a marketing plan. Most advertising firms have a market research department that can help you develop survey questionnaires and analyze and interpret the data. The drawback to using a professional consulting and advertising firm is the cost. Find a consultant or advertiser who will analyze and interpret the data and help you develop a marketing plan for a nominal fee.

---

* www.sba.com

CONCLUSION

After completing all of the necessary requirements, Happy Home Child Learning Center opened on March 4, 1994, with two children and two full-time teachers. I only had $2,500.00 left in savings, which would be used to pay my teachers. I did not pay myself a salary for the first five months after starting my business. For the next four weeks, I went on an aggressive marketing campaign. I was fortunate, but I would never wait that long again to start marketing my center. Many people who were on the waiting list at my in-home childcare center did not want to go to a center because it was much larger.

After thinking about what their fears were, I decided to invite my entire waiting list to "an Open House" on a Saturday. Many people were so impressed by how clean and well organized the center was that they registered on the spot. I created savvy marketing tactics like offering registration discounts if they signed up by a certain date. This worked well, and soon word of mouth proved to be the best marketing tool.

Within a few short months, we were at full enrollment. Each room was well equipped, and our staff continued to grow. Nine years later, we have over 102 children, with a waiting list over eight months long. We have sixteen full-time employees, one food server, a full-time clinical licensed social worker, and a maintenance person. We own all of our equipment and a school bus. We are accredited by the NAEYC. More importantly, our children are thriving, growing, and succeeding. Two poems that our children learn when they arrive at our school are "Dreams" by Langston Hughes and "It Couldn't Be Done" by Edgar Guest. Our poems, proverbs, hands-on curriculum, and the excellent teachers that I have been blessed to have on my team are what I am most proud of. I truly believe that you become what you are by the choices you make.

If you have already envisioned yourself opening your own childcare center, the only thing left to do is to **Step Out on Faith and Do It!**

THE END

Appendix A
Sample Parent
Handbook

CREATING A PARENT HANDBOOK

Your parent handbook should contain all of the rules and regulations listed below:

☐ Program Statement
- ✓ Hours of Operaion
- ✓ Closings
- ✓ Snow Days

☐ Distribution of Enrollment
- ✓ Ratios
- ✓ Number of Classrooms

☐ Admissions Procedures
- ✓ Registration and Pre-Admission Form (Application)
- ✓ Pre – Admission Interview
- ✓ Tuition and Fees

☐ Additional Charges
- ✓ Breakfast
- ✓ Late Tuition Fees
- ✓ Late Pick-Up Fees
- ✓ Return Check Fees

☐ Program Statement
- ✓ Hours of Operation
- ✓ Closings
- ✓ Holidays and Teacher Work Days
- ✓ Snow Days

☐ Attendance
- ✓ Vacation
- ✓ Staff Child Ratios

☐ Nutrition
- ✓ Food Policy
- ✓ Diet Restrictions

☐ Transportation
- ✓ Safety Policy
- ✓ Field Trips

☐ Items From Home
- ✓ No toy policy
- ✓ Extra Change of Clothing
- ✓ Books always welcomed

☐ Dress Code
- ✓ School Uniforms

☐ Family Involvement
- ✓ Parent Quarterly Meetings
- ✓ Parent/Teacher Conferences
- ✓ Parent Workshops
- ✓ Fund-Raising Events
- ✓ Procedure for Parent Concerns
- ✓ Information Updates
- ✓ School Newsletter
- ✓ Classroom Newsletter

☐ Discipline Policy
- ✓ Guidelines for Appropriate Behavior

☐ Medical Requirements

- ✓ Immunizations and Physicals

☐ Health Standards

- ✓ Guidelines for Illness
- ✓ Communicable Diseases

☐ Procedure for Administering Medication

- ✓ Registering Medication
- ✓ Procedure for Completing Forms

☐ Accidents and Injuries

- ✓ Procedure

☐ Emergency Information

- ✓ Daily phone numbers
- ✓ Emergency contacts in case parents cannot be reached

☐ Authorization to pick–up child

☐ Daily Report

☐ Hygiene

☐ Naptimes

☐ Outdoor Play Periods

☐ Field Trip procedure

☐ Birthday Parties

☐ Holiday Parties

☐ Graduation

☐ Procedure for Disenrolling a Child

☐ Termination of Enrollment

Parent Handbook

Train up a child in the way he should go,
And when he is old, he will not depart from it

Proverbs 22:6

TABLE OF CONTENTS

OVERVIEW..63

WELCOME 64

OBSERVED HOLIDAYS 65

PROGRAM STATEMENT 66

1   HOURS OF OPERATION...66

    1.1   Closings...66

    1.2   Snow Days 66

2   DISTRIBUTION OF ENROLLMENT 66

3   ADMISSIONS PROCEDURES 67

    3.1   Registration and Pre-admission Form (application)...........................67

    3.2   Pre-Admission Interview 67

4   FEES 67

    4.0.1   Additional Charges 68

    4.0.2   Before and After Care 68

    4.0.3   Late Penalties 68

    4.0.4   Vacation 68

    4.0.5   Return Check Policy 68

5   STAFF-CHILD RATIO 69

6   ATTENDANCE 69

7   NUTRITION 69

    7.1   Food Policy..69

    7.2   Diet Restrictions..69

8   ARRIVAL AND DEPARTURE...70

    8.1   Late Arrival - Absences 70

    8.2   Toddler, Preschool and Kindergarten 71

9   TRANSPORTATION POLICY 71

    9.1   Transportation Safety Policy 71

10   ITEMS FROM HOME 71

11   CLOTHING 72

11.1 Toddlers: 72

11.2 Preschoolers: 72

11.3 Appropriate School Dress Code 72

    11.3.1 STANDARD UNIFORMS 72

        2 Years to 3 Years 72

        4 years to 5 years 73

12 FAMILY INVOLVEMENT 73

12.1 All Parents Meeting (3X per school year) 73

12.2 Procedures for Parent/Guardian Concerns 74

12.3 Information Update 74

12.4 Discipline 74

12.5 Birthday and Holiday Parties 75

12.6 Graduation 75

13 MEDICAL REQUIREMENTS 75

13.1 Immunizations and Physicals 75

13.2 Health Standards: Guidelines for Illness..............................76

13.3 Health Standards: Regulations for Medication 77

13.4 Procedures for Registering Medication.................................77

14 ACCIDENTS OR INJURIES 78

15 EMERGENCY INFORMATION 78

16 AUTHORIZATION TO PICK UP CHILD 78

17 DAILY REPORT 79

18 HYGIENE 79

19 NAP TIMES 79

20 OUTDOOR PLAY PERIODS..79

21 FIELD TRIP PROCEDURE..80

22 TERMINATION OF A CHILD FROM ENROLLMENT 80

23 PROCEDURE FOR DISENROLLING A CHILD 81

National Organizations 113

OVERVIEW

Deborah L. Tillman founded Happy Home Child Learning Center in 1994 out of a deep respect for young children in knowing that in a positive, supportive environment, they can flourish. Happy Home is geared toward educating and guiding children between the ages of 1 through 5. The emphasis focuses on cultivating self-esteem, self-discipline, social relations, and physical and mental growth.

OUR PHILOSOPHY

Happy Home is a center with vast visions. Our goal is to be a proactive force in the lives of young children. We believe that each child is a unique and special person with individual, physical, social, emotional, intellectual needs and abilities. Our child-centered program focuses on the development of a positive self-image and fulfillment of each child's potential. In a conducive environment, with appropriate equipment and supplies, enriching experiences are provided with emphasis on sensory and perceptual skills; language development; concept formation problem solving; and abstract thinking. Each child is encouraged to explore and develop by a warm, understanding and capable staff. Through our working relations with the City of Alexandria Social Services and other community- based organizations, we will be able to create extensive programs that consolidate a pool of expertise.

Deborah L. Tillman, M.S. Ed
Executive Director

WELCOME

Welcome to Happy Home Child Learning Center! We are happy to enroll you and your child into our program.

This manual of policies and procedures should serve as a guide for your full and active participation.

Understanding the great impact that home and family have on a child's development and the fact that a child's first teachers are his parents, we solicit your cooperation and support in making this joint effort between home, workplace, and school a happy and meaningful experience for all. Our center takes the first step in supporting and caring for your children. We hope you, as parents, will join us in our efforts.

Deborah L. Tillman, M.S. Ed
Executive Director

OBSERVED HOLIDAYS

NEW YEARS DAY

MARTIN LUTHER KING'S BIRTHDAY

WASHINGTON'S BIRTHDAY

GOOD FRIDAY

MEMORIAL DAY

INDEPENDENCE DAY

STAFF IN-SERVICE WORK DAY

Last three days in August

LABOR DAY

COLUMBUS DAY

*VETERAN'S DAY

THANKSGIVING DAY

DAY AFTER THANKSGIVING

CHRISTMAS EVE

CHRISTMAS DAY

NEW YEARS EVE

*VETERAN'S DAY - TEACHER PLANNING DAY

PROGRAM STATEMENT

1 HOURS OF OPERATION

The Happy Home Child Learning Center operates from 7:00 a.m. to 6:00 p.m., five days a week.

- Child drop off is between 7:00 a.m. - 9:00 a.m.

- Child pickup is between 4:30 p.m. - 6:00 p.m.

- No child regardless of phone call, appointment etc., will be allowed to enter the school after 12:00 p.m.

- There is an open door policy for all families.

1.1 CLOSINGS

Happy Home is closed on weekends, all Federal Government holidays, the Friday after Thanksgiving, and if Christmas Eve or New Year's Eve is on a Friday. When Christmas Eve falls on a weekday, other than Friday, Happy Home will close at 2:00 p.m. When New Year's Eve falls on a weekday, other than Friday, Happy Home will close at 4:00 p.m. Graduation, the Center will close at 1:00 p.m. A list of observed holidays is enclosed. Teacher workdays are the last Wednesday, Thursday and Friday in August.

1.2 SNOW DAYS

The Center does not close for extreme weather conditions unless the Federal Government completely closes down. However, Happy Home reserves the right to close in extreme weather conditions regardless of the Federal Government of there is a majority vote by the Parent Advisory Board that weather effects the health and safety of all children.

2 DISTRIBUTION OF ENROLLMENT

Happy Home Child Learning Center accepts children age 12 months through 8 years of age. The Center has a present licensed capacity for 45 children at any one time. The children are placed in the following age groupings:

- Infant Toddlers   12 to 18 months
- Toddlers   18 to 30 months
- Preschoolers   2 ½ to 3 ½ year olds
- Preschoolers   4 to 5 year olds

A child will be moved from one group to the next as his chronological age, emotional maturity social and physical development make the change feasible. Availability of space in each classroom is another consideration. Every effort will be made to discuss with parents the transitions of children from one class to the other. However, the Administrator makes the final decision about placement.

3 ADMISSIONS PROCEDURES

Application for admission should be made at the Center. Acceptance will be on a first come, first-serve basis depending upon space available in the classroom serving the age group of the child and a pre-admission interview.

3.1 REGISTRATION AND PRE-ADMISSION FORM (APPLICATION)

This form contains pertinent information about the parent(s), which is used for consideration of entrance into the program.

3.2 PRE-ADMISSION INTERVIEW

The Administrator upon the receipt of the application will contact parents. If a space is available, an interview with the applicant will be scheduled for further consideration and evaluation. If a space is not available, the child will be placed on the waiting list and notified when an opening does occur.

4 FEES

Registration Fee	$65.00 non-refundable	
Re-registration Fee	$65.00 non-refundable	
Security Deposit	$150.00 non-refundable	
Weekly Fees	**Without Breakfast**	**With Breakfast**
Children 12 months to 30 months	$190.00 per week	$198.00 per week
Children 2 ½ to 5 years	$170.00 per week	$178.00 per week

All weekly fees are to be paid every Friday, one week in advance for the following week prior to the child entering the learning center. Please take note: If Friday falls on a holiday, all childcare fees are due on Thursday. Exception -- Thanksgiving fees are to be paid on Wednesday.

Breakfast is $8.00 per week to be paid at the beginning of each month.

4.0.1 Additional Charges

$5.00 will be charged for every day weekly fees are late. This fee is to be paid immediately upon notification. Weekly fees are to be considered late after 6:00 p.m. on Friday.

4.0.2 Before and After Care

$80.00 per week **(Transportation not provided)**

4.0.3 Late Penalties

$1.00 per minute will be charged from 6:01 p.m. until 6:10 p.m.

$2.00 per minute from 6:11 p.m. until 7:00 p.m.

After 7:00 p.m., authorities will be notified if we have not heard from the parents. *This fee must be paid at the time of arrival or before your child can return to school.*

Christmas Eve
$10.00 will be charged every minute after 2:01 p.m.

New Years Eve
$10.00 will be charged every minute after 4:01 p.m.

Graduation
$10.00 will be charged every minute after 1:00 p.m.

4.0.4 Vacation

When your child is going to be out for a vacation, you **must** give the center at least 48 hours written notice and pay for the weeks that your child will be out.
*All fees are to be paid year around to reserve a space for your child. Your vacation, trip times and absences due to illness are not exempt.

4.0.5 Return Check Policy

There will be a $50.00 returned check policy fee to be paid to the Center in addition to the original childcare fee, which was agreed to. All fees will be due in cash on the first day upon returning to the child learning center, after the center has notified the Applicant of its return; and The Center has the discretion to re-deposit a check at the parent's request. However, the parent must pay any fees that were incurred from the return check.

The Center will not accept any future checks from the Applicant (upon notice of any returned check) and will not provide any further services to the Applicant until full payment is received.

5 STAFF-CHILD RATIO

In compliance with the licensing regulations of the State of Virginia the following pupil-teacher ratios are adhered to. Many of the ratios are better than mandated by the state:

Number of Staff	Number of Children	Age
1	4	12-18 months
1	5	18-30 months
1	7.5	2 1/2-3 1/2 years
1	8	4-5 years
1	10	6-8 years

6 ATTENDANCE

Tuition is based on a five-day week and full tuition will be charged for one through five days of attendance.

7 NUTRITION

A balanced diet and planned nutritional meals and snacks are provided for all children.
We follow USDA standards for nutrition. Meals and snacks for all children are served as follows: From 7:00 a.m. to 8:00 a.m. (Breakfast), 10:00 a.m. (Snack), 11:00 a.m. Session #1, 11:30 a.m. Session #2, 12:00 p.m. Session #3. (Lunch). 2:30 p.m. Session #1, 3:00 p.m. Session #2, 3:30 p.m. Session #3 (Afternoon Snack).

7.1 FOOD POLICY

Absolutely NO food is to be brought into the Center except **when requested** or a special occasion, such as a party, a recital or if your child is on a special diet, vegetarian, or has an allergy. For those special times you supply food, we encourage you to choose nutritional rather than "junk" foods. Check with your child's teacher for suggestions and arrangements. In addition, all items must be store bought.

7.2 DIET RESTRICTIONS

Please note on the child's registration form any restrictions that should be placed on the child's diet. These restrictions should be updated with a written dated and signed request from the parent and physician. We want to help in any way so that your child remains healthy.

8 ARRIVAL AND DEPARTURE

Each child enrolled in the Center's program must be formally checked-in by the Supervisor in charge. This check-in incorporates parent's signing in, a general inspection of the child and for any noticeable symptoms of illness or related problems. The Center is required by law to report any <u>suspicion</u> of child abuse to the proper authorities. The parent should volunteer any information regarding possible symptoms of illness involving the child or family.

All children **must** arrive by or before 9:00 a.m. unless we have received a phone call prior to 9:00 a.m. indicating that you will be late for the day. If we do not receive a phone call and the parent arrives after 9:00 a.m., on the 3rd violation, your child will not be admitted to school. Exceptions will only be made for unforeseen circumstances i.e. (traffic, accidents, incidents). The parent should also take this opportunity to note any special instructions of a temporary nature such as a deviation from the daily schedule or diet plan. Etc. If the child is returning to the Center upon recovering from an illness, the parent must bring a Physician's Clearance if the illness was a communicable nature. All children are protected when each child comes to the center in good health.

8.1 LATE ARRIVAL - ABSENCES

If a child will be arriving after 9:00 a.m. the parent must phone the Center's Administrator or staff member. If this procedure is not followed on the 3rd violation, the child will not be admitted to enter the center for that day.

If a child is late more than two times in one week or six times in a thirty-day period, the Center will send a late warning notice to the parent. If there are extenuating circumstances, the parent should discuss the situation with the Administrator. The Administrator then makes the final decision about the time of arrival.

If there is no progress within the next ten days, the Center will give a two-week notice to disenroll the child.

If a child will not be in the Center on a given day, the parent must call the Center. Every effort should be made to make doctor appointments etc., before 10:00 a.m. so that the child can arrive at the Center no later than 12:00 p.m.

If a child is not picked up by 7:00 p.m. the Center will have to contact the local authorities.

We know that consistency is good for young children and we want all the children to participate in as much of the program as possible.

8.2 TODDLER, PRESCHOOL AND KINDERGARTEN

The child is to be accompanied into the Center by an adult and left in the presence of a staff member. All parents must sign their child in and out each day. The child should never under any circumstances be allowed to enter the building alone. Also, the child should not be left inside the door of the Center to find his or her own way. All children must be delivered to a staff member, by the Parent or Guardian and a daily health check and information exchanged be performed at that time. If this regulation is not complied with then you are placing both the child and the Center in a compromising position. Each of us wants to protect and support our children.

9 TRANSPORTATION POLICY

The Center does not provide daily transportation to and from the Center.

9.1 TRANSPORTATION SAFETY POLICY

The majority of the Center's field trips will be held during summer camp, the summer season months June through August. Transportation to the field trips will be by a licensed school bus.

All state safety regulations will be adhered to. Parents will be notified of any field trips at least two weeks in advance. Parents will periodically be asked to attend at least one field trip throughout the Child Learning Center's year.

10 ITEMS FROM HOME

Children are encouraged to leave any personal items (such as toys) at home for several reasons: the Center cannot be responsible for any personal items; personal toys often cause dissension and jealousy among the children; and a child is often unnecessarily upset if his/her toy cannot be located when he/she is ready to go home. All of these circumstances can be prevented by simply discouraging the child from bringing his/her own things since the center has ample toys and equipment for all of the children.

However, if the child does have a book, record or a tape that he/she would like to share with his/her class, he/she may bring it to school providing that it is clearly labeled with the child's name and arrangements are made with the child's teacher. Please do not allow the child to bring guns, war toys or other items relating to aggression or destruction. If a child needs a special object to help ease a transition between home and childcare, please discuss this special case with the Administrator.

11 CLOTHING

11.1 TODDLERS:

Parents should provide a bag for the child, which contains at least one change of clothing, and two or three pairs of underwear. All clothing and bags should be clearly marked with the child's name. Children in diapers are required to wear disposable diapers.

11.2 PRESCHOOLERS:

All preschool children have individual cubbies. The parent should provide a snapshot of the child so that his/her space can easily be identified. All exterior clothing such as coats, sweaters, hats and mittens should be clearly marked with the child's name and placed in his/her cubby upon arrival. Parents should also provide at least one complete change of clothing in a clearly labeled bag. This clothing will be kept at the Center and used should the child soil his/her clothing. All soiled changes of clothing should be removed from the Center and replaced with another clean set of clothing as needed.

Note: If you have any outgrown children's clothing, we would appreciate your donation to supplement our collection.

11.3 APPROPRIATE SCHOOL DRESS CODE

Children are required to wear school uniforms. The school uniform reduces competition and places the emphasis on what a child can become on the inside, not what he or she is wearing on the outside.

>Uniforms can be purchased from Robcyns
>3660 King Street (Bradlee Shopping Center)
>Alexandria, Virginia 22302
>(703) 379-7800

11.3.1 STANDARD UNIFORMS

2 Years to 3 Years

Winter:	HHCLC Royal Blue Sweat Suits
Spring/Summer:	Royal Blue Shorts White and Royal HHCLC T-Shirts
Socks:	Plain white socks

Shoes:	Students should wear shoes at all times (no sandals). For uniformity, shoes must be predominately white sneakers with white shoelaces OR predominately black sneakers with black shoelaces, no cartoons, flowers, gadgets or graphics.

4 years to 5 years

Boys:	Navy Blue Trousers Light Blue Long Sleeve Polo Shirt
Socks:	Plain, navy or white socks
Girls:	(When kneeling, hemline must touch the floor)
Blouse:	Blue Peter Pan Collar
Socks:	Plain navy or white socks or tights

From November 1ˢᵗ until April 30ᵗʰ plain white turtle neck shirts may be worn in place of blouses.

Children are required to dress in their school uniforms at all times unless otherwise noted by the center administrator. One violation will result in a warning, the second violation will result in a final warning and the third violation will result in non- admittance to the school for the day.

> *Coming together is a beginning,*
> *Staying together is progress*
> *But working together is a Success*

12 FAMILY INVOLVEMENT

Parent/Teacher Conferences. Both parent/guardian and child must attend conferences to meet with teachers to go over child's progress report.

Failure of parent/guardian to attend a scheduled parent teacher conference will result in your child not being allowed back into school until an appointment is rescheduled.

12.1 ALL PARENTS MEETING (3X PER SCHOOL YEAR)

- ♦ Back to School Night – Last Tuesday in September (HH #2) and last Wednesday in September (HH #1)
- ♦ New Year's Meeting (All Parents) January
- ♦ All Parents Quarterly Meeting (April)

73

All parents/guardians are required to attend the scheduled "January Parent Meetings". If you cannot attend, a representative must attend in your place. During these meetings parents have the opportunity to learn more about school procedures and policies and become actively involved in further developing both personal and the schools mission.

Failure of Parent/Guardian or Representative to attend a meeting will result in a $10.00 to go toward future supplies. Parental involvement is vital to the success of the school and the child. Failure to become involved will result in your child being removed from the school.

12.2 PROCEDURES FOR PARENT/GUARDIAN CONCERNS

If a parent has a concern or disagreement they should: Discuss the matter with the teacher and attempt to resolve the disagreement through an informal discussion. If there is no resolution to the problem, the parent/guardian should contact the Director. The Director will mediate the problem with all parties involved.

12.3 INFORMATION UPDATE

The parent is responsible for notifying the Center of any change of pertinent information contained in the Registration forms. Simply indicate the information to be changed, and turn the sheet into the office. The Center is responsible for obtaining current information on all enrollees, and it is impossible to do that without the help of the parent. Monthly newsletters are provided for parents in order to keep them updated.

12.4 DISCIPLINE

Discipline and guidance shall be consistent and based on an understanding of the individual needs and development of a child and shall be directed toward teaching the child acceptable behavior. Children shall not be the subjected to harsh or cruel treatment. Children shall not be humiliated or subjected to abusive or profane language. "Punishment shall not be associated with food, napping or toilet training. Bedwetters shall not be shamed or treated in a punitive manner." (Division of Licensing Minimum Standards). Rather, the child will be helped to understand why his/her conduct is unacceptable and what is acceptable in a given situation. Brief supervised separation from the group will be used when appropriate.

If the behavior of a child becomes radical or destructive, the parent will be consulted concerning appropriate methods of discipline or available sources of assistance.

The school and each individual classroom will operate under a positive and "proactive" discipline system that encourages children to make good choices. Discipline and guidance shall be encouraged and based on an understanding of what is appropriate.

12.5 BIRTHDAY AND HOLIDAY PARTIES

The Center invites parents to bring birthday cakes, cookies or party favors for a child's birthday party. The teacher can provide the parent with the approximate number of classmates in a child's class. Please discuss the arrangements with your child's teacher at least a day in advance of any special event. Birthday cakes must be store or bakery brought. If any characters are going to appear at the party, the name, address, phone number should be discussed with the Administrator at least 24 hours in advance. All parties begin at 3:30 P.M., unless otherwise notified.

The Center also tries to conduct parties on Valentine's Day, and Christmas. Parents may volunteer to bring treats for a child's class to add to the celebration that the teacher has planned. Again, please discuss your plans with your child's teacher or Administrator at least a day in advance of these events.

12.6 GRADUATION

In order to participate in the June Graduation, each child must be five years of age by or before September 30th.

13 MEDICAL REQUIREMENTS

13.1 IMMUNIZATIONS AND PHYSICALS

The child shall have a medical examination by a licensed physician who can certify the following items that the child:

- ◆ is free from transmissible infections and contagious disease:
- ◆ is physically and mentally capable of participating in a regular program of child care activities: and
- ◆ has received all immunizations appropriate for the child's age level.
  (The parent will be required to update the immunization records as needed.)

Virginia licensing standards require that we have these records on file and that they be current.

13.2 HEALTH STANDARDS: GUIDELINES FOR ILLNESS

The child must meet certain daily health criteria for daily attendance at the Center. The child will not be admitted if he/she is known to have exhibited any of the following symptoms in the preceding 24-hour period:

- ◆ Temperature elevations greater than 100 degrees (oral);
- ◆ Rash or blisters of face and/or trunk that are deemed contagious:
- ◆ Two or more loose stools in one hour or three loose stools in three hours:
- ◆ Contagious cough:
- ◆ Persistent lethargy:
- ◆ Discharge from eyes, nose or any body orifice:
- ◆ Swelling apparent in any area of the body whether accompanied by fever or not:
- ◆ Excessive vomiting (spontaneous and/or within one-half hour of feeding):
- ◆ Diarrhea

If any of the above symptoms are observed while the child is in attendance at the Center, the parents (guardians) will be notified immediately and will be expected to arrange for the child to be picked up within one hour. (See next page).

Any child who has been absent due to disabling illness or a communicable disease or absent for two (2) or more days will only be readmitted to the Center upon receipt of a signed statement by a non-related licensed physician that he/she is healthy and non-contagious.

Below is a list of communicable diseases and the duration of time that your child must be excluded from school. A letter must accompany all conditions below from the physician indicating child is not contagious.

- ◆ Ringworm (skin)   24 hours on medication (Lotrimin, Tinactin, etc.)
- ◆ Ringworm (scalp)   48 hours on oral medication.
- ◆ Pinkeye   24 hours on eye medication
- ◆ Ear Infection   24 hours on antibiotic
- ◆ Cold or Flu with yellowish or discolored discharge from the nose
                       24 hours of medication
- ◆ Chicken Pox   7 days to 10 days.
- ◆ Eczema   A physician's note must be presented to the Administrator indicating that the child has eczema.

13.3 HEALTH STANDARDS: REGULATIONS FOR MEDICATION

The following regulations for administering medication are adhered to:

1. The Center is under no obligation to administer medication of any kind and may refuse to give medication if the Administrator or Supervisor-In-Charge feels that it is not appropriate.

2. The Center will not administer any medication such as Kaopectate, or other anti-diarrhea medication whether is it prescription or otherwise.

3. The Center will not administer Tempra. Tylenol, aspirin or other fever-control medications since the child should not be in attendance at the Center if he/she has had a temperature elevation in the preceding 24-hour period. (Please see Infection Control Policy).

4. Since the child should not be in attendance at the Center if he/she has shown symptoms of illness, it should not be necessary for the Center to administer medicine except under certain conditions such as allergy medicine or medicine that must be taken for an extended period of time. THIS TYPE OF medicine WILL BE GIVEN UNDER THE SET OF CRITERIA LISTED BELOW:

   ◆ With physician's prescription

   ◆ **NO MEDICATIONS FOR THE CONTROL OF FEVER OR DIARRHEA WILL BE GIVEN BY THE CENTER**

   ◆ The only medications given will be those that are prescribed by a physician. The medication must be in the original container with label and must not be left at the center overnight.

   ◆ If medication needs to be given longer than 10 days, a physician's medication form must be given.

13.4 PROCEDURES FOR REGISTERING MEDICATION

The following procedures for registering medications are adhered to:

1. Completely fill out one or more of the Medication Request Forms.

2. Present medicine to Supervisor-In-Charge. (Please do this in person in case there are any questions.)

3. If the physician has written a clearance for more than three days or if the label specifies that the medication is to be "given for an approximate time_____ on _____ day" indicate the appropriate number of days and present this information to the Supervisor-In-Charge.

4. The medication will be given as directed as long as the circumstances comply with the Center's written guidelines.

14 ACCIDENTS OR INJURIES

In the event of an accident causing recognizable symptoms, first aid treatment will be administered by the Supervisor-In-Charge. An incident report will be filled out on each occurrence and a notation made in the child's permanent record. If the accident is of a serious nature, the parent will be notified immediately.

If the accident requires emergency hospitalization, all will be called to transport the child to Alexandria Hospital.

All enrollees are covered by Hartford Pre-School Accident Program and are entitled to benefits as specified by our policy. A copy of this policy is on file in the office. There will always be someone at the Center who has had First Aid and CPR Training.

15 EMERGENCY INFORMATION

The Center shall be informed of the telephone number or numbers at which a parent can be reached at all times. The parent should have an emergency number of someone other than himself or herself to notify in case the parent cannot be reached.

16 AUTHORIZATION TO PICK UP CHILD

The child will be released to either the parent(s) or guardian and those persons listed on the registration form. If the child is to be released to any person other than those listed above, the parent should contact the Supervisor-In-Charge and leave the necessary information either by telephone request or in writing. The person authorized to pick up may be required to present a picture I.D. Also, no person under the age of 18 will be allowed to pick-up a child from the center. If there are any special circumstances, please discuss the issues with the Administrator.

17 DAILY REPORT

A daily report will be filled out for children 1 to 3 years of age. The purpose of this form is to provide a means of communication with the parent on a daily basis. It will keep the parent informed of the child's general health routine while at the Center. The form will be placed on the child's name in his/her classroom.

18 HYGIENE

Children through five years of age receive frequent face and hand washings, and their clothing will be change if it becomes overly soiled providing that the parent has furnished a clean change of clothing. All 4 and 5 year olds are required to bring a toothbrush with the child's name on it and encased. Children brush teeth after the last snack.

19 NAP TIMES

Children over 18 months receive an afternoon nap from 12:00 p.m. to 2:00 p.m., 12:30 p.m. to 2:30 p.m. or 1:00 p.m. to 3:00 p.m. These periods of time are provided in the interest of maintaining good health standards and physical development of the child. Any special blanket to be used by the children should be properly labeled when brought to the Center and taken home each week for washings. Although the Center makes every effort to keep up with the children's belongings (providing they are properly labeled), we cannot assume responsibility for any items brought to the Center). The Center provides cot sheets for all enrolled children. Pillows are not allowed.

20 OUTDOOR PLAY PERIODS

Most of the children involved in the Center's program are in attendance on the basis of a nine-hour day. Approximately one hour of that time is spent in outdoor playtime. This time is very important for a growing child because the child's body not only needs exercise but also needs improved physical coordination and gross motor skill development. Children benefit from being outdoors during all seasons.

Sometimes, a parent may feel that certain weather conditions may be harmful to a child's health in other ways. However, if a child is dressed appropriately with a hat, coat, mittens, sweater, galoshes, scarf, etc. then he/she should be able to play outside in almost any weather conditions (except when raining).

If a child is too ill to go outside, then perhaps he/she may be too ill to be at school. However, if special permission is desired concerning a child's staying inside during inclement weather, then the parent should bring a signed and dated written request to the Supervisor-In-Charge each day that permission is needed. The reason for this request should be stated in writing.

21 FIELD TRIP PROCEDURE

Children under the age of 3 years old will not be allowed to attend field trips. However, the center will remain open during all field trips for children under the age of three.

22 TERMINATION OF A CHILD FROM ENROLLMENT

The Center may terminate a child's enrollment effective immediately, if any of the following conditions occur:

♦ In the judgment of the Center's Administrator, the child's behavior threatens the physical or mental health of other children and staff members in the Center.

♦ Childcare fees are not paid within five days after payment is due.

♦ Late fees are not paid within 24 hours after due.

♦ If a child is ill when brought to the Center and the parent fails to promptly pick up a sick child when called within a timely manner.

♦ All other situations must be accompanied by a two-week notice from the Administrator.

♦ The parent may terminate the child's enrollment only upon a two (2)-week written notice to the Administrator. If this termination policy is not adhered to, the parent will be subject to a civil suit and/or attorney's fees.

♦ Before there is a final decision, every effort will be made to discuss alternatives with parents.

23 PROCEDURE FOR DISENROLLING A CHILD

The teacher and Administrator are aware of the problem and initial here_____

The Parent, Teacher and Administrator have a meeting to notify the parent of a problem and alternatives are discussed. Parent initials here_____

Administrator/Teacher initials_____

Parent is given a two-week notice if possible, unless any of the exceptions from the policy manual apply.

Date and alternatives discussed_____

_____ ☐_____

Parent initial's here_____

Administrator/Teacher initial's here _____

Copy of this form is given to the parent.

Appendix B
Sample
Employee Handbook

CREATING AN EMPLOYEE HANDBOOK

Your employee handbook should contain information similar to what is listed below.

☐ Welcome Letter

☐ Purpose of the Handbook

☐ Overview of the Child Care Center

- ✓ Background Information
- ✓ Mission Statement

☐ Code of Business Practices

- ✓ Statement of Confidentiality
- ✓ Preparation
- ✓ Food
- ✓ Phone Calls

☐ Equal Employment Opportunity

- ✓ Reasonable Accommodation
- ✓ Harassment
- ✓ Minimum Age Requirements

☐ Recruitment and Selection

- ✓ Criminal Record Checks
- ✓ Child Protective Services/ Department of Social Services
- ✓ Sworn Disclosure Statements

☐ Compensation

- ✓ Weekly/Bi-Weekly
- ✓ Overtime
- ✓ Holidays
- ✓ Workshops
- ✓ Vacation
- ✓ Benefits
- ✓ Bereavement

☐ Inclement Weather

- ✓ Federal Government Policies
- ✓ Regarding Snow Days
- ✓ School Delays

- ☐ Open Communication
  - ✓ Regarding Complaints
  - ✓ Regarding Suggestions
  - ✓ Parent Concerns
- ☐ Company Dress Code
  - ✓ Workplace Environment
  - ✓ Creating a positive environment
  - ✓ Smoke Free
  - ✓ Drug Free
- ☐ Employee Policy Forms
  - ✓ Contract
  - ✓ Disciplinary Actions
  - ✓ Termination of Employment

Employee Handbook

Train up a child in the way he should go,
And when he is old, he will not depart from it

Proverbs 22:6

TABLE OF CONTENTS

1 CODE OF BUSINESS PRACTICES 90

   1.1 Policy 90

   1.2 Preparation 90

   1.3 Food 90

   1.4 Phone Calls 91

2 EQUAL EMPLOYMENT OPPORTUNITY 91

   2.1 Policy 91

   2.2 Guidelines 91

      2.2.1 Reasonable Accommodation 91

      2.2.2 Harassment 91

      2.2.3 Minimum Age Requirements 91

3 RECRUITMENT, SELECTION AND OFFERS OF EMPLOYMENT 92

   3.1 Policy 92

   3.2 Selection Process 92

   3.3 Offers of Employment 92

4 TIME SHEETS AND PAY PERIODS 92

   4.1 Policy 92

   4.2 Purpose and Scope 92

   4.3 Major Responsibility Assignments 92

   4.4 Pay Period and Paychecks Guidelines 93

      4.4.1 Paydays 93

5 VACATION 93

   5.1 Policy 93

   5.2 Purpose and Scope 93

   5.3 Eligibility 93

   5.4 Guidelines 94

6 INCLEMENT WEATHER 94

   6.1 Policy 94

   6.2 Guidelines 94

   6.3 Snow Days 94

7 EMPLOYMENT OF RELATIVES 95

   7.1 Policy 95

    7.2   Purpose and Scope...95

    7.3   Definitions..95

8   OPEN COMMUNICATION...95

    8.1   Policy..95

    8.2   Definitions..95

    8.3   Responsibility 95

9   SEXUAL HARASSMENT 96

    9.1   Policy..96

    9.2   Purpose and Scope...96

10 HOLIDAY PAY...96

    10.1 Policy..96

    10.2 Guidelines 96

11 BEREAVEMENT 97

    11.1 Policy..97

    11.2 Purpose and Scope...97

    11.3 Definitions..97

    11.4 Guidelines 97

12 COMPANY DRESS CODE..97

    12.1 Policy..97

    12.2 Guidelines 98

13 OVERTIME COMPENSATION 98

    13.1 Guidelines 98

14 SMOKE-FREE WORKPLACE...98

    14.1 Policy..98

    14.2 Purpose And Scope..98

    14.3 Guidelines 98

15 DISCIPLINARY ACTIONS 99

    15.1 Policy..99

    15.2 Purpose and Scope...99

    15.3 Definitions..99

    15.4 Guidelines 99

    16.1 Policy..100

16.2 Purpose and Scope 100

16.3 Definitions 100

16.4 Discharge for Cause 101

16.5 Reduction in Force 101

16.6 Delivery of Materials upon Employment Termination 101

17 EMPLOYEE ORIENTATION 102

17.1 Policy 102

17.2 Purpose and Scope 102

18 FIELD TRIPS 102

18.1 Policy 102

19 FIRE AND EMERGENCY 102

19.1 Policy 102

19.2 Monthly Procedure 102

19.3 Building Fire Alarm Procedure 102

DOCUMENTATION OF ORIENTATION FOR NEW EMPLOYEES, AS REQUIRED BY MINIMUM STANDARDS FOR LICENSED CHILD DAY CENTERS 103

1 CODE OF BUSINESS PRACTICES

1.1 POLICY

Since its founding in 1994, Happy Home has followed the policy of developing its business on the basis of quality service and integrity in dealing with its parents and others. The code of Business Practices sets for the important principles of business conduct that support basic policy and should be followed by all Happy Home employees.

This Manual is to be strictly followed at all times and under all circumstances. Any violation will subject an employee, without regard to position with the corporation to disciplinary action.

In addition to complying with the specific provisions of this code, all employees are expected to adhere to high ethical standards in conducting company business. Happy Home also expects each employee to meet all of the ethical obligations of his or her profession. The company's reputation and the best interest of the employees require that the corporation maintain business practice standards that will command the respect of everyone with whom the company deals.

Confidentiality - as part of their duty of loyalty to the corporation, all employees must maintain the confidentiality of the parents, children and co-workers. Employees should never disclose corporation information of any kind to others unless they are certain that disclosure is appropriate and has been authorized. Equal care must be taken to keep confidential any proprietary information of parents, children and others entrusted to the corporation. (Confidentiality Statement is enclosed).

1.2 PREPARATION

All employees are expected to be prepared, and focused for work. Weekly Lesson plans are due to the Director no later than 2:00 p.m. on Fridays. If Friday is a holiday, Lesson plans will be due on the Thursday before the holiday.

1.3 FOOD

When working directly with children no food or coffee or soft drinks are allowed. Exceptions during snacks and lunches, employees are encouraged to eat with the children in order to foster good eating habits. Drinking water is allowed at all times in a plastic cup.

1.4 PHONE CALLS

Personal phone calls are not allowed. All calls should be made during employee's personal time. Exception: Emergencies.

2 EQUAL EMPLOYMENT OPPORTUNITY

2.1 POLICY

It is the policy of Happy Home to provide equal opportunity to all employees and all applicants for employment without regard to race, sex, religion, age, national origin, U.S. military veteran status or handicap status.

2.2 GUIDELINES

2.2.1 Reasonable Accommodation

In keeping with Happy Home Child Learning Center's commitment to provide a productive work environment in an atmosphere free of bias or discrimination the company:

♦ Shall make reasonable accommodation for employees who may wish to follow certain religious observances or practices when such accommodations can be made without undue hardship to the conduct of Company business.

2.2.2 Harassment

Employee conduct involving verbal or physical harassment based on color, race, national origin, age or sex will not be tolerated and may subject the employee to disciplinary action, including termination. Conduct is considered harassment when it:

♦ Has the purpose or effect of creating an intimidating, hostile or offensive work environment;

♦ Has the purpose or effect of interfering with an individual's employment opportunities; or

♦ Adversely affects an individual's employment opportunities.

2.2.3 Minimum Age Requirements

According to the Division of Licensing Minimum Standards all employees must be 18 years of age or older to be considered for employment.

Any employee who believes that he or she has been the subject of discrimination should contact Mrs. Tillman, Director of Admissions, (703) 931-1051.

3   RECRUITMENT, SELECTION AND OFFERS OF EMPLOYMENT

3.1   POLICY

It is the policy of Happy Home to staff positions with the most appropriately qualified personnel giving full consideration to qualified employees within the Company, or to recruit and employ qualified individuals from outside of the Company as needed to maintain and enhance a quality work force.

3.2   SELECTION PROCESS

When a position becomes available, qualified personnel will be notified. Applicants from outside of the company are screened. A more extensive interview follows and an in class observation completes the selection process. This process also applies to advancement within the Company.

3.3   OFFERS OF EMPLOYMENT

All offers of employment are made prior to orientation which will be outlined in the offer letter.

4   TIME SHEETS AND PAY PERIODS

4.1   POLICY

It is the policy of Happy Home to require accurate and timely reporting of all hours worked.

4.2   PURPOSE AND SCOPE

This policy outlines the guidelines for the accurate and timely preparation and submission of time sheets and applies to all Happy Home employees.

4.3   MAJOR RESPONSIBILITY ASSIGNMENTS

Employees are responsible for completing time sheets accurately, (entering hours daily) completely, and submitting them in a timely manner. When you arrive each day employee should sign in and when you leave each day employee should sign out. If you do not sign in or out for the day, you will not be paid for that day.

The Director is responsible for reviewing time sheets to ensure their accuracy and completeness, and for ensuring that all employee's are familiar with policies and practices related to completion of time sheets.

4.4 PAY PERIOD AND PAYCHECKS GUIDELINES

4.4.1 Paydays

Paydays are every other Friday. Direct Deposit is encouraged. If payday falls on a holiday employees will be paid before the holiday. Any changes would occur only due to the discretion of and upon direction from the Board of Directors.

5 VACATION

5.1 POLICY

It is the policy of Happy Home to provide each employee with an annual vacation entitlement as paid time off away from work.

5.2 PURPOSE AND SCOPE

To provide a traditional paid time off benefit that will allow employees to enjoy a break in year-round routine. This policy applies to all Happy Home full-time, employees.

5.3 ELIGIBILITY

An employee cannot receive entitlement to earned vacation time until he/she has satisfactorily completed the 90-day probationary period in addition to the one year at Happy Home.

Vacation time will not be extended to any employee that meets or exceeds 25 absences in the calendar year.

Unused vacation time will not be extended from year to year. You must use or loose.

Because of our strenuous school year, vacations should be taken during the months between July and August.

Two weeks before a scheduled vacation, employee must submit to the Director for approval lesson plans schedules and content for the days you will be out.

5.4 GUIDELINES

The Company prefers that employees take one vacation period of at least five consecutive days.

Selection of vacation dates is subject to the approval of the employee's Director. Preference in selection of dates will be granted based on length of employee's services.

Happy Home encourages all employees to make every effort to schedule appointments before or after work hours. However, we realized that there may be times when it may be impossible to do so. Request for leave must be completed if more than 1/2 hour is needed away from employment. All requests must be made at least 24 hours in advance or will be denied. (Request for leave from enclosed)

6 INCLEMENT WEATHER

6.1 POLICY

Happy Home recognizes that severe weather conditions occasionally occur, and that employees must know what is expected of them with respect to reporting to work. Happy Home's policy routinely corresponds to that of the federal government but ultimately will be determined by the Director.

6.2 GUIDELINES

In the event of severe weather conditions, Happy Home employees should listen to the local news and weather broadcasts for the area in which they work. Employees should follow the federal government with regard to closures. Exceptions to this may be authorized by the Company Director. Happy Home will make every effort to inform employees by phone and leave messages on the center's answering machine regarding closures.

6.3 SNOW DAYS

When the Federal Government closes you will not be paid for a snow day.

When the Federal Government is open and Happy Home closes you will be paid for the snow day.

7 EMPLOYMENT OF RELATIVES

7.1 POLICY

It is the policy of Happy Home to consider all qualified candidates for employment, including close personal relatives of existing Happy Home employees, provided that such employment does not create an inequitable or disruptive working relationship.

7.2 PURPOSE AND SCOPE

This policy establishes guidelines regarding the employment of close relatives for either full-or-part-time employment.

7.3 DEFINITIONS

A relative, for purposes of this policy, is defined as a member of the immediate family (e.g., siblings, parents, children, grandparents, etc.) and spouses.

8 OPEN COMMUNICATION

8.1 POLICY

It is the policy of Happy Home to encourage communications between Management and employees, to solicit employee's ideas and suggestions about the Company, and to ensure that employee complaints are equitably resolved.

8.2 DEFINITIONS

A complaint, for purposes of this policy, is defined as an alleged violation misinterpretation or inequitable application of Happy Home's policies, practices, or procedures.

8.3 RESPONSIBILITY

The Director is responsible for maintaining an open and receptive environment that encourages employees to provide ideas and suggestions about the Company and that fosters resolution of employee complaints.

Employees are encouraged to provided input regarding the Company's policies and business practices, and are responsible for voicing their concerns to the Director in a timely fashion.

9 SEXUAL HARASSMENT

9.1 POLICY

It is the policy of Happy Home to recognize and enforce the right of employees to work in an environment that is free of sexual harassment. The Company will not tolerate verbal or physical conduct by an individual, including employees, and parents, that harasses, disrupts and interferes with an employee's work performance by creating a sexually intimidating, offensive, or hostile work environment.

9.2 PURPOSE AND SCOPE

The purpose of this policy is to describe and affirm Happy Home's position prohibiting sexual harassment in the work place. This policy applies to all employees in all operating units of Happy Home.

10 HOLIDAY PAY

10.1 POLICY

It is the policy of Happy Home to provide additional compensation or compensatory time off to employees who are required to work on scheduled holidays.

10.2 GUIDELINES

In order to receive holiday pay, employees must be in a pay status both the last working day before and the first working day after the holiday. When a holiday falls within an employee's personal leave, the day(s) off will charged to holiday and not to vacation.

Happy Home observes the following schedule:

- New Year's Day

- M.L. King's Birthday

- President's Day

- Good Friday

- Memorial Day

- Independence Day

- Labor Day

- Columbus Day

- Veterans' Day (Employee Work Day)

- Thanksgiving Day

- Friday after Thanksgiving

- Christmas

11 BEREAVEMENT

11.1 POLICY

It is the policy of Happy Home to grant paid leave time and benefits to employees who are required to take time off from work due to death in their immediate family.

11.2 PURPOSE AND SCOPE

This policy outlines the guidelines for providing salary and benefits to employees who are required to take time from work due to death in their immediate family.

11.3 DEFINITIONS

Immediate family: Immediate family shall be defined as father, mother, husband, wife, son, daughter, grandmother, grandfather, sister and brother.

11.4 GUIDELINES

Up to three days leave with full pay will be granted to any full-time non-probationary employee who suffers a death in their immediate family upon written request to the Director. Any additional time will be deducted from the employee's annual leave. Any exceptions to this policy must be approved by Company Director.

12 COMPANY DRESS CODE

12.1 POLICY

It is the policy of Happy Home to have our employees project a professional, positive image of the Company by wearing appropriate business attire during regular business hours.

12.2 GUIDELINES

Generally, appropriate attire shall include pants, blouse, shoes, skirt, or dress. Happy Home Smocks should be worn at all times while working. Name badges must be worn when the Center is expecting guests. You will be given at least 24 hour notice by the Director. Jeans, sneakers, shorts, will only be allowed during some field outings. Skirts above the knee will not be allowed. For special events such as; Christmas, concerts, and graduations, all staff employees must wear semi-formal attire. For each event, the Director will coordinate attire with staff.

13 OVERTIME COMPENSATION

13.1 GUIDELINES

Overtime hours must be approved in advance and shall be recorded in the pay period in which they are worked and shall be paid on the corresponding pay day. Overtime hours shall not be carried forward to a subsequent pay period.

14 SMOKE-FREE WORKPLACE

14.1 POLICY

It is the policy of Happy Home to restrict the smoking of tobacco products on Happy Home operated facilities.

14.2 PURPOSE AND SCOPE

The purpose of this policy is to outline Happy Home guidelines for implementation and maintaining a smoke-free workplace.

14.3 GUIDELINES

Happy Home is committed to providing a safe, comfortable, and productive work environment. Therefore, smoking is prohibited in and around Happy Home.

15 DISCIPLINARY ACTIONS

15.1 POLICY

It is the policy of Happy Home to take appropriate disciplinary action as required to maintain a productive and professional work environment and to ensure adherence to the company's policies and procedures.

15.2 PURPOSE AND SCOPE

The purpose of this policy is to outline the guidelines and procedures for taking disciplinary action and applies to all employees in all operating divisions of Happy Home.

15.3 DEFINITIONS

At the discretion of Happy Home Management, progressive discipline is the approach implemented in any particular case through which employees are involved and, as appropriate, disciplined for unsatisfactory performance or behavior or for instances of misconduct and given the opportunity to correct them.

Suspension is a disciplinary action requiring the employee to stay away from the work place, with or without pay.

15.4 GUIDELINES

Fairness in the treatment of employees is essential to sustain a productive and professional work environment. This policy outlines the guidelines for taking disciplinary steps, including, at Management's discretion, progressive discipline intended to provide employees with the opportunity to correct behavior or performance so that the employment relationship can continue.

Areas that may warrant disciplinary action (including immediate dismissal) include, but are not limited to, the following:

- Unacceptable performance
- Unauthorized or excessive tardiness or absence
- Insubordination
- Security breaches

- Theft/misuse of funds
- Time sheet or expense reporting inaccuracy
- Conflict of interest
- Violation of Company policies

The specific action to be taken, up to and including immediate termination, will be based on the nature of the problem, the seriousness of the violation, and or possible consequences of the employee's behavior to Happy Home.

The action to be taken may be a:

- Verbal warning

- Written warning

- Second written warning accompanied by appropriate disciplinary action (e.g., suspension and/or establishment of a probationary period)

- Termination

16 TERMINATION OF EMPLOYMENT

16.1 POLICY

It is the policy of Happy Home to consider all employees to be employed-at-will who may terminate their employment who may be terminated at anytime with or without cause, to the extent permitted by law.

16.2 PURPOSE AND SCOPE

This policy establishes the guidelines and procedures for terminating an individual's employment, and applies to all employees in all operating units of Happy Home.

16.3 DEFINITIONS

Voluntary termination is termination of employment that is initiated by the employee. For voluntary termination company must receive a two weeks notice. Involuntary termination is termination of employment that is initiated by the Company. Failure to submit a two-week notice will subject the employee to pay a fine of $1,000.

Employee signature

Discharge for cause is defined as involuntary termination of employment as a result of an employee's breach of Company policy, law or ethics. A discharge for cause may be initiated by the Company due to, but not necessarily limited to, the following reasons:

- Extensive tardiness
- Unacceptable performance
- Conflict of interest
- Insubordination
- Misconduct
- Physical or verbal abuse to Company employees or children
- Use of alcoholic beverages in the work place
- Use, possession, sale, manufacture or distribution of illegal chemical substances in the work place

- Timesheet misrepresentation
- Security violation
- Theft
- Concealment of material facts in order to secure employment.
- Excessive absences and tardiness
- Absence without phone call (exception employee must be hospitalized, verification is necessary)
- Distributing materials to parents without prior-approval from the Director

16.4 DISCHARGE FOR CAUSE

An employee who is discharged for cause shall be dismissed from employment immediately upon notification. If an employee is discharged for cause, the Director shall supervise the employee's removal of personal belongings and escort the employee from the work place.

16.5 REDUCTION IN FORCE

When workload requires that the number of employees be reduced, the Management shall consider the following factors in determining how the work force will be reduced.

- Overall performance
- Duration of time at Happy Home

16.6 DELIVERY OF MATERIALS UPON EMPLOYMENT TERMINATION

Immediately upon the end of Employee's employment with Happy Home Inc. employee shall deliver all correspondence, drawings, lesson plans, books, papers and documents in the possession or control of Employee to Happy Home Inc.

17 EMPLOYEE ORIENTATION

17.1 POLICY

It is the policy of Happy Home to provide all new employees with an orientation program to familiarize them with the organization and to prepare them to perform their jobs.

17.2 PURPOSE AND SCOPE

This policy is for the orientation of new employees. This orientation applies to all operating units of Happy Home. (Orientation form enclosed)

18 FIELD TRIPS

18.1 POLICY

All field trips are taken by the whole center. No one is left here for communication purposes. However, the center does have 24 -hour answering machine.

19 FIRE AND EMERGENCY

19.1 POLICY

Monthly false fire drills will be conducted in order to better prepare the staff and children in the event of "a real" fire.

19.2 MONTHLY PROCEDURE

Upon hearing a fire bell employees are instructed to immediately proceed with children to nearest exit doors leading to the outdoor play area.

19.3 BUILDING FIRE ALARM PROCEDURE

Upon hearing a fire alarm outside of the center all employees are instructed to proceed with (Happy Home #1 only) children out of their immediate classroom doors to the left exit and outdoors. All Bathrooms, closets, etc. must be checked. Remember, the safety of the children is most important.

Happy Home
Child Learning Center, Inc.

DOCUMENTATION OF ORIENTATION FOR NEW EMPLOYEES, AS REQUIRED BY MINIMUM STANDARDS FOR LICENSED CHILD DAY CENTERS

Name of Employee:_____ Date: _____

Prior to assuming job responsibility all staff shall receive:

_____ Center's operating information including all information provided to parents as listed in Standard (2.14.1)

_____ Policy for Arrival and departure of Children. (2.14.2)

_____ Programs and Policies about Appropriate Discipline, Food Policies, and Transportation. (2.14.3)

_____ Procedures for Storing and Administering Medications. (2.14.4a)

_____ Policy for Reporting Child Abuse or neglect to the appropriate local department of social services (Note: Section 63.1248.3 of the Code of Virginia requires any person providing full or part-time child care for pay on a regularly planned basis to report suspected child abuse or neglect.) (2.14.4.b)

_____ Procedures for caring for late arrival children. (2.15.1)

_____ Procedures to confirm absence of a child (2.15.2)

_____ Procedures to monitor children's location during field trips (2.15.3)

_____ Procedures for lost children, medical emergencies, and other disasters (2.15.4)

_____ Individual responsibilities in the event of fire, including the location and operation of any fire extinguisher and fire alarm boxes. (7.27)

_____ Job responsibilities and supervisor. (3.14.1)

_____ Playground safety plan. (3.14.3)

_____ Confidential treatment of personal information. (3.14.4)

_____   Minimum Standards for Licensed Child Care Centers as related to the staff person's responsibilities. (3.14.5)

_____   Center's Policy on acceptable and unacceptable discipline methods. (6.67 as it relates to 6.59-6.66)

_____   _____

Date Orientation Completed   Signature of Employee

                                    _____

                                    Date Orientation Completed

104

Appendix C
List of Resources

When developing a list of resources, I am often asked what books I read in order to plan and develop the childcare center. To be perfectly honest, I couldn't find any books that gave me a step-by-step process for how to open a center. However, I did find many resources that were inspirational. I have included them in the next few pages.

Based on the letters, emails and telephone calls, I have compiled list of resources for your convenience.

TEN LESSONS LEARNED:

- Be patient, passionate and persistent
- Invest in a good grant writer, lawyer and accountant **early**
- Be Proactive instead of Reactive
- Communicate well
- Learn to delegate
- Focus on strengths
- Surround yourself with people who are smarter and wiser than yourself
- Never compromise your morals, values, high expectations and goals
- Take initiative to make it happen
- Share your knowledge with all of those who are willing to listen

KEY PHRASES I LIVE BY:
- Seek God First
- Let go and Let God
- Live Your Purpose
- With God ALL THINGS ARE POSSIBLE ~ Philippians 4:19

INSPIRATIONAL CHILDREN'S BOOKS
- The Little Engine That Could ~ Watty Piper
- The Giving Tree ~ Shel Silverstein
- Waiting For Wings ~ Lois Ehlert
- In the Box ~ Toni Morrison

📖 Good Night Moon ~ Margaret Wise Brown

📖 Chicka, Chicka Boom Boom ~ Bill Martin Jr., & John Archabault

📖 Good Night, God Bless ~ Susan Heyboer O'Keefe

📖 The Honest to Goodness Truth ~ Patricia C. McKissack

📖 The Big Box ~ Toni Morrison

📖 How are you peeling? ~ Saxton Freymann

📖 Red Leaf, Yellow Leaf ~Lois Ehlert

ADULT BOOKS: THAT HAVE MADE A DIFFERENCE IN MY LIFE

📖 Give It to Me Straight ~ Pastor Lyle Dukes

📖 Maya Angelou ~ I know why the caged bird sings?

📖 Values ~ Marva Collins

📖 The Seven Habits of Highly Successful People ~Stephen R. Covey

📖 No Excuses ~ Samuel Casey Carter

📖 Tomorrow's Children ~ Riane Eisler

📖 Maximize the Moment ~T.D. Jakes

📖 Beyond Fear ~ Don Miguel Ruiz

📖 Rich Dad Poor Dad ~ Robert T. Kiyosaki

📖 Think Big ~ Ben Carson, MD

📖 The Millionaire Next Door ~ Thomas Stanley & William Danko

📖 The Out of Sync Child ~ Carol Stock Kranowitz

📖 Acts of Faith ~ Iyanla Vanzant

📖 Making a Difference ~ Craig R. Fiedler

📖 Self Reliance ~ Ralph Waldo Emerson

📖 Speak to my Heart God ~ Kay Arthur

📖 Guide My Feet ~ Mariam Wright Edelman

Excellence is not an Act, but a habit
~Aristotle

Things which matter most must never be at
the mercy of things which matter least
~Goethe

The significant problems we face cannot be solved at the same level
of thinking we were at when we created them.

I am what I am today because of the choices I made yesterday

No one can hurt you without your consent
~Eleanor Roosevelt

What lies behind us and what lies before us are
tiny matters compared to what lies within us.
~ Oliver Wendell Holmes

Everybody can be great because everybody can serve
~ Martin Luther King Jr.

No weapon that is formed against thee shall prosper
~Isiah 54:7

God has not given you the spirit of fear,
"but of power, and of love, and of a sound mind"
(2 Timothy 1:7)

Only as far as I see can I go;
Only as much as I dream can I be;
Only as high as I reach can I grasp;
~Benjamin Mayes

When God wants an important thing done in this world or a wrong
righted, He goes about it in a very singular way. He doesn't release
thunderbolts or stir up earthquakes. God simply has a tiny baby
born, perhaps of a very humble mother. And God puts an idea in the
baby's mind, and then God waits. The great events of this world are
not battles and elections and earthquakes and thunderbolts. The
great events are babies, for each child comes with the message
that God is not yet discouraged with humanity, but is still expecting
goodwill to become incarnate in each human life.
~ Edmond McDonald, Presbyterian Outlook

INSPIRATIONAL POEMS

- ◆ DREAMS ~ Langston Hughes

- ◆ IN VAIN ~ Emily Dickerson

- ◆ STILL I RISE ~ Maya Angelou

- ◆ IT COULDN'T BE DONE ~ Edgar Guest

- ◆ DON'T QUIT ~Jill Wolf

- ◆ INVICTUS ~ William Ernest Henley

DREAMS   BY LANGSTON HUGHES

Hold fast to dreams
For if dreams die
Life is a broken-winged bird
That cannot fly

Hold fast to dreams
For if dreams go
Life is a barren field
Frozen in the snow

EMILY DICKERSON

If I can stop one Heart from breaking
I shall not live in vain
If I can ease one life the Aching
Or cool one pain
Or help one fainting robin
Unto his nest again
I shall not live in Vain

STILL I RISE BY MAYA ANGELOU

You may write me down in history
With your bitter, twisted lies,
You may trod me in the very dirt
But still, like dust, I rise.

Does my sassiness upset you?
Why are you beset with gloom?
'Cause I walk like I've got oil wells
Pumping in my living room.

Just like moons and like suns,
With the certainty of tides,
Just like hopes springing high,
Still I'll rise.

Did you want to see me broken?
Bowed head and lowered eyes?
Shoulders falling down like teardrops,
Weakened by my soulful cries?

Does my haughtiness offend you?
Don't you take it awful hard
'Cause I laugh like I've got gold mines
Diggin' in my own backyard.

You may shoot me with your words
You may cut me with your eyes,
You may kill me with your hatefulness,
But still, like air, I'll rise.

Does my sexiness upset you?
Does it come as a surprise?
That I dance like I've got diamonds
At the meeting of my thighs?

Out of the huts of history's shame
I rise
Up from a past that's rooted in pain
I rise
I'm a black ocean, leaping and wide,
Welling and swelling I bear in the tide.

Leaving behind nights of terror and fear
I rise
Into a daybreak that's wondrously clear
I rise
Bringing the gifts that my ancestors gave
I am the dream and the hope of the slave
I rise
I rise
I rise

IT COULDN'T BE DONE BY EDGAR GUEST

Somebody said that it couldn't be done,
But he with a chuckle replied,
That "maybe it couldn't" but he would be the one
Who wouldn't say so till he tried.
So he buckled right in with the trace of a grin
On his face, if he worried he hid it.
He started to sing as he tackled the thing
That couldn't be done, and he did it.

Somebody scoffed: "Oh, you'll never do that;
At least no one ever has done it",
But he took off his coat and he took off his hat,
And the first thing we knew he'd begun it.
With a lift of his chin and a bit of a grin,
Without any doubting or quid it,
He started to sing as he tackled the thing
That couldn't be done, and he did it.

There are thousands to tell you it cannot be done,
There are thousands to prophesy failure.
There are thousands to point out to you one by one,
The dangers that wait to assail you.
But just buckle in with a bit of a grin,
Just take off your coat and go to it.
Just start in to sing as you tackle the thing
That couldn't be done, and you'll do it.

DON'T QUIT BY JILL WOLF

Don't quit when the tide is lowest,
For it's about to turn
Don't quit over doubts and questions,
For there is something you may learn
Don't quit when the night is its darkest
For it's just a while till dawn
Don't quit when you've run the farthest,
For the race is almost won
Don't quit when the hill is steepest
For the goal is almost nigh
Don't quit, for you're not a failure
Until you fail to try

INVICTUS BY WILLIAM ERNEST HENLEY

Out of the night that covers me,
Black as the pit from pole to pole,
I thank whatever gods may be
For my unconquerable soul.

In the fell clutch of circumstances
I have not winced nor cried aloud.
Under the bludgeonings of chance
My heart is bloody, but unbowed

Beyond this place of wrath and tears
Looms but the horror of the shade,
And yet the menace of the years
Finds, and shall find, me unafraid.

It matters not how strait the gate,
How charged with punishments the scroll,
I am the master of my fate:
I am the captain of my soul.

NATIONAL ORGANIZATIONS

Child Care Action Campaign
330 7th Ave, 18th Floor
New York, New York 10001
(212) 239-0138

The Child Care Employee Project
6536 Telegraph Road
Oakland, CA 94609
(415) 653-9889

The Child Care Food Program (CCFP)
U.S. Department of Agriculture
Washington, DC 20250

The Child Care Law Center
22 Second Street 5th Floor
San Francisco, CA 94105
(415) 495-5498

The Children's Defense Fund
122 C Street NW Suite 400
Washington, DC 20001
(202) 628-8787

The Children's Foundation
725 15th Street, NW, #505
Washington, DC 20005
(202) 347-3300

Council for Early Childhood Professional Recognition
1718 Connecticut Ave., NW, Suite 500
Washington, DC 20009
(202) 265-9090

Mothers at Home
8310 Old Court House Road
Vienna, VA 22182

National Association for the Education of Young Children
1834 Connecticut Ave NW
Washington, DC 20009-5786
(202) 232-8777

National Black Child Development Institute
1463 Rhode Island Ave., NW
Washington, DC 20005
(202) 387-1281

National Center for Clinical Infant Program
2000 14th Street North, Suite 380
Arlington, VA 22201

National Commission on Working Women
1325 G Street NW
Washington, DC 20005
(202) 273-5764

Save the Children Child Care Support Center
1340 Spring Street. NW #200
Atlanta, GA 30309
(404) 885-1578

United States Department of Agriculture
Mercer Corporate Park
300 Corporate Boulevard
Robbinsville, New Jersey 08691-1598
(609) 259-5139

Work and Family Information Center
The Conference Board
845 Third Ave
New York, NY 10022
(212) 759-0900

Virginia Small Business Financing Authority
Child Day Care Financing
901 East Byrd Street
Richmond, Virginia 23206-0798
(804) 371-8184

Made in the USA
Monee, IL
20 January 2023

25794558R00076